INCULTURATION

Working Papers on Living Faith and Cultures

edited by

Arij A. Roest Crollius, S.J.

XI

This issue has been published in collaboration with the Secretariat of the International Federation of Catholic Universities, Paris.

CENTRE "CULTURES AND RELIGIONS" - PONTIFICAL GREGORIAN UNIVERSITY

JEAN DUCRUET, MARCELLO AZEVEDO, GREGORY G. BAUM,
ARIJ A. ROEST CROLLIUS, FRANCISCUS X. SEDA,
GUILLERMO RODRIGUEZ IZQUIERDO

FAITH AND CULTURE
THE ROLE OF THE CATHOLIC UNIVERSITY

ROME – PARIS
1991

1989 – First edition
1991 – First reprint

ISBN 88-7652-604-8

EDITRICE PONTIFICIA UNIVERSITÀ GREGORIANA
Piazza della Pilotta, 35 - 00187 Roma

Brief Curriculum Vitae of Speakers

DUCRUET, Jean

President, Université Saint Joseph, Beirut, Lebanon

Born in 1922 in Bourg en Bresse, France
Studies in Law, Philosophy, Theology, Economics (doctorate)
Entered Society of Jesus in 1942

Professor of Economics at the Université Saint Joseph
Director of Political Sciences Institute
Vice-Chancellor Faculty of Law and Economics, and Chancellor
President of Université Saint Joseph since 1975

Publications (selected):
- "Les Capitaux Européens au Proche-Orient"
- articles in professional journals: "Proche-Orient, Etudes Econo-
  miques", "Aggiornamenti Sociali", "Revue de l'Action Populaire",
  "Le Commerce du Levant".

AZEVEDO, Marcello

Research Fellow at the Center John XXIII for Social Research and
Action in Rio de Janeiro, Brazil

Born in 1927 in Belo Horizonte, Brazil
Studies in Philosophy, Anthropology, Theology
Doctorate in Missiology at the Gregorian University, Rome
Entered the Society of Jesus in 1957

Director of Studies at the Brazilian College in Rome
Provincial of one of the Jesuit Provinces in Brazil
Senior member at the Woodstock Theological Center at Georgetown Uni-
versity, Washington, USA

Publications:
- "Modernidade e Cristianismo"
- "Inculturation and the Challenges of Modernity"
- "Comunidades Eclesiais de Base e Inculturação da Fé"
- "Educacion, Sociedad, Justicia"

BAUM, Gregory G.

Professor of Religious Studies at McGill University, Montréal, Canada

Born in 1923 in Berlin, Germany
Studies in Mathematics, Physics, Theology and Sociology

Professor of Theology and Religious Studies at St. Michael's College, Toronto
Appointed to Department of Sociology at the University of Toronto, Canada
Editor of "the Ecumenist"
Member of editorial committee of "Concilium"

Books published:
- "Faith and Doctrine"
- "Religion and Alienation"
- "Truth Beyond Relativity: Karl Mannheim's Sociology of Knowledge"
- "Ethics and Economics"

ROEST CROLLIUS, Arij A.

Director, Centre for Religions and Cultures, Gregorian University

Born in 1933 in Tilburg, Netherlands
Joined the Society of Jesus in 1952
Studies of Philosophy, Theology and History of Religions

Assistant Professor of Philosophy at the Coptic Seminary, Cairo
Professor in History and Theology of Religions, Pontifical Gregorian University
Dean, Faculty of Missiology, Gregorian University

- Author of studies on questions regarding Scriptural Monotheism
  and Cultural Pluralism in English, French, German, Italian, Arabic,
  Spanish, Dutch.

SEDA, Franciscus Xaverius

President of the Atma Jaya Foundation and Chairman of the Board of Directors of the Atma Jaya Catholic University

Born in 1926, in Maumere, Flores, Indonesia
Studies of Economy at the Catholic University of Tilburg, Netherlands
Married, two daughters

Minister of Plantation, of Agriculture, of Finance, of Transportation, Communications and Tourism
Ambassador in Brussels to the European Economic Communities and the Kingdom of Belgium and Luxemburg
General Chairman of the Catholic Party
Member of the Advisory Council of the Democratic Party of Indonesia (P.D.I.)
Founder of the Catholic University Atma Jaya in 1961
Dean of the Economic Faculty of UNIAKA
Member of Pontifical Commission "Justitia et Pax" in Rome

TABLE OF CONTENTS

PREFACE

INCULTURATION welcomes the Thematic Report of the Jakarta Assembly of the International Federation of Catholic Universities as Nr. XI of the series of Working Papers on Living Faith and Cultures. Thanks to this gracious collaboration with I.F.C.U., INCULTURATION is now published for the first time also in a Spanish and French edition. In order to keep down the costs of publication, the typographic format has been simplified.

The theme of the Jakarta Assembly fits in extremely well with the perspective of our series. We are glad to give wider publicity to these papers, which demonstrate both theoretical depth and practical realism.

Other seminars and workshops on the theme of inculturation are being prepared by the Research Center of IFCU. In due time we hope to be able to publish the study papers and the results of these international meetings.

Arij A. ROEST CROLLIUS, S.J.

INTRODUCTION

Faith and Culture, the Role of a Catholic University, providing a spiritual concern in the cultural context: such is the broad, yet far-reaching purpose of the theme as examined by the 16th General Assembly in Jakarta from August 1 to 5, 1988.

This topic was undertaken as a contribution to the World Decade for Cultural Development 1988-1997 as celebrated under the auspices of United Nations Organizations and Unesco.

The approach adopted was prepared by international teams and by a world-wide questionnaire sent to all member institutions of the IFCU. The results of that enquiry are reflected in the papers of this report. In the panelists' communications, the effort and services provided in Catholic Universities are equally well illustrated. It is our hope that this will stimulate other universities to open up or to improve their programmes of teaching, research and extracurricular activities in this realm.

This publication includes most of the papers and communications given at the Jakarta Assembly.

An in-depth report has been published separately by the Catholic University of Louvain **"Faith and Culture at the Catholic University of Louvain"** which is the outcome of a collective reflection organized by the CODI (Council for Integrated Development).

Also released separately are the papers of a workshop by students and faculty on the topic **"The Catholic University as a Bridge between Peoples of Different Cultural Backgrounds in Asia: A Practical Example"** directed by Daniel ROSS, S.J. of Fu Jen Catholic University in Taiwan.

Lucien MICHAUD
Secretary General, IFCU

Original: French

THE CHRISTIAN FAITH

IN A SITUATION OF CULTURAL PLURALISM

by Jean DUCRUET
Beirut, Lebanon

The problems which arise from the expression and reception of God's revelation in the plurality of human cultures are to be found throughout the entire Church's history from the first Council of Jerusalem to Vatican II. The problems have a different tone according to the regions and the times, and the preoccupations of the Churches in Africa are not those of the churches in Europe nor in Latin America. Each one of us puts forth the cultural status of the faith with one's own background and one's own feelings. I shall not be different from others and I prefer to situate well my environment while recognizing that other environments would justify a different presentation of this theme, God's revelation in the plurality of human cultures.

We, in Lebanon and in the Middle East, live in general in a plurality of churches: - plurality of Catholic liturgies which differ in the Maronite, Greek, Chaldean, Syriac, Armenian, Latin or Coptic churches, often co-existing in the same city; - plurality of theologies (the Oriental theologies are less influenced than the Latin by analytical methods, they are less attracted to a synthesis of Revelation and Philosophy, they make less distinction between the world of knowledge and that of life; they emphasize differently the dogmas); - plurality of rules (the ordination to priesthood of married men for example does not present any difficulty in the Oriental Churches, and the appointment of Bishops by the Pope is a rarity). We do not suffer the inconveniences of a monolithic Church and we find cultural pluralism perfectly normal in the Church. We live on the other hand in a region which has been profoundly influenced by the division of the Church's body, orthodoxy and catholicism; and this division is due in part to incomprehensions of cultures. We are therefore more aware than others of the risks of schisms. Finally we live in a region where were born and where coexist Judaism, Christianity and Islam. We are therefore vitally concerned by the encounter of religions and cultures in a historical context when they insert and express themselves.

It is with reference to this Middle East context that I shall speak of the cultural status of revelation before offering a few thoughts on this matter within the university setting which is already one of cultural pluralism and will become more and more so.

I - THE CULTURAL STATUS OF THE REVELATION

The Christian revelation seems to me to be characterized by three features which are inseparable: a) transcendance (salvation in Christ is neither within reach of human cultures nor commensurate to them; b) historicity (salvation is achieved in a historical manner by events and within a continuity which does not exclude a dialogue of cultures); c) universality (salvation is destined to all mankind, it is open to all cultures).

1. TRANSCENDANCE OF REVELATION AND HUMAN CULTURES

The transcendant character of the Revelation flows from the twofold fact that God reveals himself and that He offers us to share his divine life: "In His goodness and wisdom, God chose to reveal Himself and to make known to us the hidden purpose of His will, by which, through Christ, the Word made Flesh, man has access to the Father in the Holy Spirit and comes to share

2

in the divine nature", such is the essential of Revelation according to St. Paul to the Ephesians (1).

When it pleased God, he took Abram away from his nation, away from his gods, away from his culture; his culture was rather primitive and inoffensive compared to the high cultures of Sumer, of Babylon, of Egypt: "Leave your land, your family, the house of your Fathers and go to the land I shall show you!" (2) Just as at the beginning of humanity, just as after the Deluge which washed away all cultures, God now created a people: "I am the Lord, creator of Israël" (3). Saint Paul, in his second letter to the Corinthians, writes: "If then any man is in Christ, he is a new creature: his former things have passed away; behold they are made new!" (4) and in his letter to the Galatians: "Neither circumcision nor uncircumcision but a new creation is of any account" (5). This theme of the new creation, of the new birth, of the new life is present in all the Scriptures: it is found at the beginning of St. John's Gospel: "Who were born not of blood, nor of the will of the flesh, nor of the will of man, but of God" (6) and at the end of the Apocalypse: "Behold, I make all things new" (7). It is not possible to express more vigorously the gratuitous character of Christian Revelation, its absolute and transcendant character. It does not stem from any human culture; it is not the blossoming of any human culture; it is commensurate with no human culture. This cultural inadequacy can be felt at all levels, that of language, that of concepts, that of behaviour.

God has given us no revealed language, no vocabulary, no heavenly grammar. We have no Gospel in the aramaïc language (in which Christ spoke); we are therefore not tempted to render sacred a particular language (like the Muslims for Arabic). One day, with a Moslem, I was attending a liturgical ceremony in the arabic language. I heard him deplore the rustic aspect of the Christian arabic language compared to the revealed language of the Coran. This reminded me, in a less ambiguous situation, of the sayings of Saint Gregory of Nysse who, when reading the Bible, "would abandon hellenism for a barbaric language" (8). Or it equally reminded me of Saint Augustin in his "Confessions" who began by saying that Holy Scripture was "not worthy of comparison with the majesty of Cicero" (9). The fact is that the latin and greek of the first Christian writers was not that of the classical period, but rather that, as has appropriately pointed out Cardinal de Lubac in reference to the "barbarisms and solecisms of the Christians", the extraordinary novelty of Christianity cannot break into a language without upsetting it and without creating its own vocabulary, a vocabulary which is always inadequate (10).

If such is the case of the limits and awkwardness of language to express our faith, what then shall happen to the concepts which are perforce used to encompass Revelation, if only when they are used to shield it from erroneous interpretation. Theology's realm is that of analogies. It can never mold concepts so that they adequately convey what it wishes to say. It says by an intermediate that which cannot be circonscribed. Theology corrects its statements by negating them. It tones down one representation by another. It destroys its image by other images (11). The theological process reminds one of the struggle of Jacob with the Angel of God: "Tell me your name". At the end of the struggle, theology is lame. "It suffers from a discrepancy between what it must say on God's behalf and the means it can use to say something to mankind" (12).

Nor does human behavior avoid this problem of a natural lack of adaptation to the evangelical revelation. That is why in the letters of Saint Paul and in the writings of the Church Fathers, the Christian is often presented as the stranger, as the non-resident, as the misfit in the local culture, as the one who has his own criteria of values, his own model "Be imitators of me as I am of Christ" (13). The Epistle to Diognete when describing the behavior of second century Christians, undoubtedly in Alexandria, underscores the non-conforming behavior of the Christian who is in this world, but is not of this world (14). The foundation of Christian values is a life in the Spirit, which Christ alone can establish. Contrary to Christianity, Islam for example does not ask its faithfuls "to be perfect as your Heavenly Father is perfect" (15). For Islam believes that Christians set standards that are too high by requiring of mankind things which cannot be reasonably obtained naturally (e.g. the pardon of injuries, the love of enemies, preference given to poverty, to celibacy...). Islam proposes an ideal in accordance with human nature and which can be reached with only the capacities of nature. There is no "grace", no participation in the life of God which would permit mankind to raise itself to the perfection of the Father.

It is important, I believe, to approach in this way the problem of the relation between faith and cultures by reminding oneself of the transcendant character of Revelation, the heterogeneity of the Evangelical message and the cultures. In order to put our cultural problem in proper perspective one must recall the "leve all" addressed to Abram, to the rich young man in the Gospel, addressed to so many martyrs, to so many converts who have felt themselves excluded from a civilization where culture and religion are one (I am thinking principally of the converted from Islam) who have found themselves culturally empoverished but who could day after Saint Paul: "For his sake, I have suffered the loss of all things and I count them as dung that I may gain Christ" (16).

2. HISTORICITY OF THE REVELATION AND HUMAN CULTURES

The second characteristic of Christian Revelation is historicity. The Christian Revelation does not have as object a religious doctrine which it behoves to each people and each time to enculturate; it does not convey a certain concept of salvation. Rather it has as object a history, that of God's intervention. It has as object the fact that salvation is given to us. Our Sacred Books are books of history, a history that is both human and divine. This in fact distinguishes the Bible from the Koran. The Koran has retained from the Bible the idea of a transcendant and holy God, who is Creator and Remunerator, but the Koran has not retained that which is the Bible's essential subject, the action of God in the world and in history. Thus it is but a message, at most a concept, the unity of God, monotheism and that explains that God should teach this truth to all peoples by a prophet taken from among themselves, according to the words of the Koran (17). Such is not the case of the Judeo-Christian Revelation: it bears on a history and this history as all histories is branded by unique happenings, situated in time and space, and by a continuity.

The events of salvation are not only unique, they also have a definitive and universal bearing; that is the Christian paradox. Pastor André Dumas appropriately reminded us of this during a colloquium organized in 1982 by the Institut Catholique de Paris with the title "Theology and Clash of Cultures". I quote: "The fundamental clash is not first of all between our different cultural pasts and presents, but with the unique pretention of Jesus to be for all and for all times the universal Christ. This clash has begun long before the incarnation, when the uniqueness of Israël was chosen by the gratuitous love of the God of the entire world" (18). The roads of salvation begin effectively in a specific history, that of a people chosen by God for a mission, that of a religious and cultural tradition matured over centuries for this purpose. No other tradition, whatever may be its value, can take the place of that tradition because it is the one chosen by God and which his Son has assumed. The Church has not been misled when it makes Christians of all cultures pray with the Psalms, which no song borrowed from other cultural heritages can replace. Or when it makes them meditate on parabols which cannot be replaced by any more recent allegorical narrative. Or when it makes them communicate an Eucharist which is not a simple ritualisation of a meal which each arranges in his own way to greet God, but which is the pascal meal, reminder of the delivrance of Israël and actualization of Christ's last Supper.

Continuity is, with the singularity of events, a constituent element of history. In an exhortation on the transmission of the Evangelical message, John Paul II said: "The Evangelical message cannot be isolated purely and simply from the culture in which it was first inserted (the biblical universe, and more specifically the cultural milieu in which Jesus of Nazareth lived) nor can it be isolated without serious losses, from the cultures in which it has found expression over the centuries. The message does not spontaneously erupt from any cultural ground; rather it is transmitted since the beginning through an apostolic dialogue which is inevitably inserted in a certain dialogue of cultures" (19). When we say transmission, one says fidelity and continuity. Today it is often said anew that the influence of hellenism on the elaboration of the faith and Christian life was great thus suggesting that the essential of the evangelical message could be extracted from its greek envelope in order to take on new forms of expression. Hans Kung for example has pointed out in his writings the opposition between the Judeo-Christian and the Christian-Hellenistic conception of the relation of Jesus to God. Kung has accepted the point of view of some authors who believe that Judeo-Christianity which has disappeared into the Christian Hellenistic Church has been continued in Islam (20). One can certainly deplore the premature disappearance of the Jerusalem Church, due principally to the fall of Jerusalem, and

even with Cardinal Danielou, believe that without this
desappearance which left too much space for the greeko
latin culture of the west, that the oriental schisms
could have been avoided (21). But one must not ignore
the considerable services which hellenism rendered to
the expansion of the Christian faith nor should we imagine
that this first dialogue of cultures entailed a rupture
or discontinuity in the transmission of faith. In this
instance, there is not marked opposition between the
Church of Jerusalem and the Pagan-Christian Church as
pointed out by Oscar Cullmann (22). In the following
period, which was so important for the definition of
dogmas, one should not be misled on the intentions of
the Church Fathers:

"It is a great illusion, writes Cardinal de Lubac,
if one believes that the intense work which brough about
the texts of Nicea, Ephesis, and Chalcedonia was
buttnessed by an effort... to adapt the wording of
Christianity to a cultural milieu different from its
original one, at the risk of hellenizing the faith
received from the first Christians... Even more so,
never did it enter their heads to refer to a systematic
deculturation or inculturation of the faith such as
invented by a few theoreticians, as if faith to pass
from one culture to another, with a writertight wall
between them, should first die, then, be born again
by some unknown process... In fact things were otherwise:
it was a continuous struggle to protect it against the
onslaughts of a hellenism which tended to swallow it
up" (23).

Judeo-Christian Revelation is a history characterized by events and by a continuity. The importance,
undoubtedly excessive, taken on by speculative theology
in the West has perhaps made us forget that an understanding of the faith is essentially an interpretation
of a history of salvation, put forth by the Scriptures
and lived by the Church and that, ultimately, it is
the reference to a set of events (Alliance, Incarnation,
Death and Resurrection of Christ, Gestures of the Holy
Spirit) and not the reference to a closed system of
truths which permit the maintenance of continuity of
faith in a dialogue of cultures.

3. UNIVERSALITY OF THE REVELATION AND HUMAN CULTURES

The third feature of Christian Revelation is universality: God intends to save all mankind. As it is

in the service of Revelation, the Church must take on
the cultural diversity of all peoples. "The Church sent
to all peoples of everytime and place is not bound
exclusively and indissolubly to any race or nation nor
to any particular way of life or any customary pattern
of living ancient or recent. Faithful to her own tradition
and at the same time conscious of her universal mission
she can enter into communion with various cultural modes,
to her own enrichment and theirs too" (24).

The requirements of a universality which respects
cultural differences and which implies a plurality in
the expression of a same faith are more and more underscored today. These requirements are perceived more
and more as the countries in Europe and North America
come to understand that "modernity" entails both
acceptance and evangelization but supposes also that
there is a type of relationship between Society and
religion which is no more that of the Christian areas.
They are perceived as such by the churches of Africa,
of Asia and of Latin America as they become conscious
of their cultural identity and of their own problems.
Finally the perception is widened as Christians of many
countries become aware of the fact that they live in
a pluricultural society and that the Church itself,
which is a pluricultural society in its own way, must
be a figure of a Kingdom to come in which God will be
all in all and where the Universal will be the communion
of respected particularities.

The **dogmatic statements** and the **theologies** which
are in relationship with them are perfectly capable
of assuming the cultural plurality. But that supposes
of course that the dogma to be understood in its nature
and function be returned to the everyday life of the
Church which in various historical circumstances probes
the mystery of the life, death and resurrection of Christ
and explains its faith. The doctrinal decisions of the
Church, being historical, are necessarily limited,
designed as they are to provide an answer to a situation
and elements of each era. Therefore theologies all the
more so are (27). It is perfectly normal that some
theologies should probe the Gospel from the point of
view of an ambiguous modernity and from the point of
view of the struggle of the poor to live decently. And
that theologies should be preoccupied by situations
where men are judged by the color of their skin, which
include women's liberation in the ecclesial thinking.
Two statements approved by the International Commission
of Theology which was created by Paul VI give insight
into this matter:

"Because of the universal and missionary character of the Christian faith, the events and words revealed by God must be each time thought out, be reformulated and lived anew within each human culture. If one wants them to bring a true answer to the questions which are rooted in the heart of each human being and that they inspire the prayers, worship and everyday life of the people of God. The Gospel of Christ thus leads each culture to its fulness and subjects it simultaneously to a creative criticism.

The dogmatic formulae must be considered as answers to specific questions and it is in this perspective that they remain true. Their ongoing interest is dependent upon the durability of the question raised. Though one must not forget that the subsequent questions which the Christians raise about the meaning of the divine Word and the conformed answers, do generate one another so that today's answers presuppose always in some way those of yesterday, though they cannot be reduced to them" (28).

The **ecclesial structures** are also perfectly able to take on the cultural plurality of peoples if only sufficient freedom of expression is left to particular churches to be active partners within the universal Church. The Church is a communion of particular churches around one of them, the Church of Rome to whom a primacy is recognized by virtue of the place it has occupied in the testimony of faith at the beginning of the Christian era. This does not make the Church of Rome a super-Church, and all the more so, the particuflar Churches are not administrative divisions of a super-Church. The Church is made up of particular churches and it is all in each. That, moreover, is why the Bishop of a particular Church has a special responsibility to it but has also a responsibility at the level of the universal Church, as underscored by the setting of Councils, of Synods, and of regional assemblies (29). Vatican II has reinstated a theology of particular churches which has remained very much alive in the Oriental Churches which have their own traditions and which has been downplayed in the Latin Church and in those regions where it has exercised its missionary activities. It is very significant that this renewal of the theology of particular Churches should have taken place at the Council in the context of the "young Churches" and their cultural dimensions:

"Thus, in imitation of the plan of the Incarnation, the young Churches (...) borrow from the customs and traditions of their people, from their wisdom and their learning, from their arts and sciences, all those things which can contribute to the glory of their Creator, the revelation of the Savior's grace, or the proper arrangement of Christian life.

"If this goal is to be achieved, theological investigation must necessarily be stirred up in each major socio-cultural area, as it is called. In this way, under the light of the tradition of the universal Church, a fresh scrutiny will be brought to bear on the deeds and words which God has made known, which have been consigned to sacred Scripture, and which have been unfolded by the Church Fathers and the teaching authority of the Church.

"Thus it will be more clearly seen in what ways faith can seek for understanding in the philosophy and wisdom of these peoples. A better view will be gained of how their customs, outlook on life, and social order can be reconciled with the manner of living taught by divine revelation. As a result, avenues will be opened for a more profound adaptation in the whole area of Christian life. Thanks to such a procedure, every appearance of syncretism and of false particularism can be excluded, and Christian life can be accommodated to the genius and the dispositions of each culture. Particular traditions, together with the individual patrimony of each family of nations, can be illumined by the light of the gospel, and then be taken up into Catholic unity" (30).

That theology and the Church structures be capable in theory, of taking on the cultural plurality of peoples does not entail that this universalism is not without problems still not fully clarified. The process of a new inculturation of Christianity ignore too much, for example, the political components and underestimates the bond between culture and religion. With regard to the political aspects suffice it to mention the case of the Libanese Christianity, which originally was a society of greco-syriac culture and which today is predominantly a society of arabic culture. This inculturation, at first accepted grudgingly, then taken on willingly, is not without riches, but has proven to be ambiguous and deceiving when arabism prove itself to be not only a culture but also an ideology in the service of pan-islamism. Lebanon has nearly lost its identity and existence in this case (31). The misunderstanding of the strength of the bond between culture and religion is much more serious: inculturation not only assumes that Christianity is dissociated from the cultures of its own origin; it also assumes that the cultures where it intends to insert itself are dissociated from the religion which frequently is at the root of these cultures and which permeates them entirely. In Thaïland, the buddhists were indignant because the Church had used in its liturgy a certain number of their sacred symbols. This is no more a time, fortunately, when one can use the ruins of Greek temples to build basilicas and inculturation should not lend itself to an accusation of "theology vandalism". That is why it is impossible to deal with the cultural status of Christian revelation without examining the relationship of Christianity with the other religions of the world.

The relationship of Christianity with other religions has been broached on three occasions by the Second Vatican Council. The dogmatic constitution on the Church, chapter 2, presents the Church as the people of God; as a gathering to which by different ways and through many modes of allegiance God calls all mankind. The Council turns its attention first to the Catholic faithful, then towards other Christians with whom "the Church recognizes that in many ways she is linked". Finally the Council looks towards those who have not yet received the Gospel but who "are related in various ways to People of God". In first place there is "the people to whom the covenants and promises were given, and from whom Christ was born according to the flesh"; "but the plan of salvation also includes those who acknowledge the Creator. In the first place among these are the Moslems who profess to hold the faith of Abraham... and those in the shadows and images who seek the unknown God, of whom God is not far distant". Finally the Council mentions "those who have not yet arrived at an explicit knowledge of God to whom Divine Providence does not deny the necessary help for salvation" (33).

The Declaration on the relationships of the Church to Non-Christian Religions deals with only the non-Christians as it was preceeded by the Decree on Ecumenism. The order of presentation is the reverse of the Declaration: the Council with the religious aspiration which is natural to human beings goes on to a brief presentation of two great religions which are more developed, hinduism and buddhism, then to Islam, then to Judaism to whom the text had been originally designed. The Council states that "the Church rejects nothing which is true and holy in the religions". It points to the dogmatic elements which are common to Christianity and Islam: One God, Creator, who reveals Himself, and who will give each man his due after raising him up. It recalls "the spiritual bond linking the people of the New Covenant with Abraham's stock". If the order of presentation in the Declaration is the reverse of that in the Constitution, the objective and the spirit are the same. "The Church looks upon what mankind has in common and urges them to live together their destiny" (34).

In these two conciliary documents, Christ, "light of people", is of course presented as he "in whom mankind must find the fulness of religious life and in whom God has reconciled all things". But it is in the Pastoral Constitution on the Church in the Modern World where in a few words explain best the universality of salvation in Christ whatever may be the religions to which one adheres: "For since Christ died for all men and since the ultimate vocation of man is in fact one and diverse, we ought to believe that the Holy Spirit in a manner known only to God offers every man the possibility of being associated with this paschal mystery" (35).

The concept of salvation thus expressed by the Council is wide and broadly encompassing. It does not artificially isolate people from the religions where they find a useful support in their quest towards God. But this concept, from the very fact that it is totally centered on Christ, and that it cannot be otherwise, does not go to the point of setting up all religions, as they are presently organized with a system of beliefs and practices, in channels of revelation and salvation, which would be parallel to the new Alliance which the Church ministers to (36). Al the more so does the Council, by the insistance it has put on pointing out that the Church, in spite of its essential novelty, is in full continuity with the Israël of yester-year, the Council therefore leaves no room for an utopian Christianity which be reborn from another matrix than that of Israël (37). On the other hand, it is important for our purpose to stress that this conciliar reminder about all the world religions puts them all in perspective, and this facilitates the dialogue.

In order to put religions in proper perspective one must maintain between religions and revelation. Religion is the human expression of the search of God;

as a human expression it is always limited, having among others certain cultural particuflarities. Revelation is an act of God, who relates to mankind. Only Christ is the absolute religion because he is completely man and completely God. That is why he is the reference, the point of discernment for the authenticity of religious experience.

"Christianity is indeed a religion of the Ultimate, an expression of faith in the ultimate revelation of God and in this context, it does not seek to complete the revelation it has received through borrowings from other religions. But because it does not pretend to be the ultimate religion, commensurate with an ultimate revelation, it does not cease to work at liberating its faith from the limits which its particular form of religion brings to it... It thus acquires the right to invite the other religions, in its wake, to seek God beyond God. And it facilitates for them the access to the revelation of which it is the bearer, by leveling the barriers of its own religious particularity... It thus becomes a universal religion..." (38).

To conclude this overview of the cultural status of revelation, and before offering a few thoughts about assuming this into a Catholic university, might I point out simply that the three features of the revelation I have reviewed, transcendance, historicity and universality, are indissociable. The unity of the faith, and the plurality of its expressions, which are consequences of the Revelation's universality, are grounded in the mystery of Christ, which, while being a mystery of universal recapitulation and reconciliation, transcends all cultures. Faith, perforce, will always express itself through religious expressions stamped by the particularities of cultures and their dialogue. But it is first of all a confession of a salvation event and it is by proclaiming this salvation event that the Church transforms the dialogue of cultures into a dialogue of salvation. By stressing in this way that the three features of revelation are inseparable, one is not of course solving easily the problems that will be raised by the evaluation of the relative importance of these three features in a real life encounter of the Christian message with a particular culture. The answers will be toned down differently taking into account the content of the culture to be evangelized, taking into account the quality of its relationship to the culture through which the message is transmitted. In the past, the culture of Alexandria for Ethiopia, the culture of Syria for

China, of Constantinople for the Slavic peoples, of Rome for the West. By reason of the historicity of revelation, there cannot be inculturation without an acculturation, that is without a meeting of two cultures (39).

II - CULTURAL STATUS OF REVELATION AND UNIVERSITY TEACHING

The Catholic universities are places where the dialogue between faith and culture is most intense, of the highest quality (40). The cultural status of the revelation is thus of direct concern to them. The Catholic universities take into account that priviledged status in the pursuit of the various functions which they take on in the service of individual persons, or societies and the Church. They do it in a number of ways often described (41) and which one need not repeat. Suffice it for me to point out that the three features of Christian revelation, namely transcendance, historicity and universality, deeply affect our attitude as Catholic universities when faced with the political, economic, scientific, cultural and religious realities which every university has to analyse as part of their mission. I will attempt it, from a particular situation, namely that of my university which has among its students, its teaching staff and its administrators, people from the sixteen ethnic-socio-religious communities which make up Lebanon. Our university recognizes itself rather well on the model of a pluralist, Catholic university described by Robert Henle for North America (42).

1. TRANSCENDANCE OF REVELATION AND UNIVERSITY TEACHING

The transcendance of God, such as understood by the Christian revelation, is compatible with and even presupposes the recognition of a certain autonomy of earthly things: "created things and societies themselves enjoy their own laws and values which must be gradually deciphered, put to use and regulated by men; then it is entirely right to demand that autonomy... it harmonizes also with the will of the Creator (43). This autonomy entails the acquisition of knowledge to master earthly realities: man must "not only respect the laws proper to each disciline, but must also acquire a true competence therein". It also entails, simultaneously, the formation of a conscience capable of putting order in the earthly things seeing it behave man "to inscribe the divine law in the life of the earthly city" (44) where it is not automatically inscribed. Man, thus faced with his responsibilities, can expect of his Christian faith principles of reflection, norms of judgement, and orientations for action. But he cannot expect specific solutions and immediate answers to his problems, these solutions being left to his discernment.

Acquisition of knowledge, formation of consciences to discernment, such are the two preoccupations of university teaching. When the inspiration of a university is Christian, the training in discernment seems to me of particular importance and it should not be neglected by limiting the objectives of the curriculum to one of technical efficiency. When a university of Christian inspiration wishes to be pluralist, it must in training for discernment respect the options of other faiths without abandoning its own options. The desire to train for discernment is desirable in all disciplines. Economics is not Christian, nor is Political Science, nor is Medicine. But there is a Christian practice in economics, in politics, in medicine. I shall not repeat here well-known considerations on the training to discernment in different disciplines (45). Rather I shall limit myself to a few examples proper to a pluricultural university and I shall review the relationship to the intellect underlying every discipline and the relationship to languages which is equally significant. I shall finally touch upon the relationship to politics.

The relationship to the intellect raises problems for a certain number of our moslem students, particularly the non-lebanese. This arises from the absolute predominance of memory over thinking/reflection stemming undoubtedly from the importance given to memorizing the Koran. This arises also from the difficulty of being critical of the matters studied whether they be historical, literary, or religious. What is of value to these students is what has been said, of all times, within a certain tradition. The value of a statement is not based on its content, its internal logic, its conformity to a system of thought but rather on the reputation of the person who transmits the message. The problem of the intellectual formation is not one of choosing this or that value nor of confrontation with it, but rather one of the scientific and critical thinking to be implemented in order to approach these values. Hence the fundamental role of all that touches on methodology, on reasoning, on objectivity. This role can only be ensured in a climate of honesty and respect. Otherwise the student will interpret these intellectual standards as a camouflaged attacks to what he considers to be his cultural heritage, which are construed to undermine it and to replace it by a western model.

The relationship to languages is equally delicate. The study of Arabic and the study of the French language take on different overtones with a Christian student and a Moslem student. The Arabic language does not have for a Christian the sacred and intangible character that it has for a Moslem. Both must become aware of Islamic religion's influence on this language. "But it is not sufficient to be aware of these links of Islam as a religion with the Arabic language and literature. One must also analyze this fact in order to sort out what belongs to each field: distinguish that which belongs to linguistics, to history of literature, to history of ideas, and that which pertains to the Moslem religion...in order to situate each field and let it be autonomous" (46). The French language does not have the same impact in every Lebanese community. For some, the French language is their language; it is part of their cultural identity and strengthens their Christian identity. For others, it is the necessary means to open up to a culture different from theirs. Finally for others, it is a simple additional means of communication which would be better received if it could be "deculturalized". It behaves to each community to assume the French language as each wishes and to each university, seeing Lebanon is priviledged in having many, to situate its programs and orientations. According to the charter, our university "proposes to promote the culture of the Arabic language and the culture of the French language as they are taken on by the Lebanese cultural identity". It tones down without coming to a full solution a situation described by a Jesuit from Irak:

"We speak the language of others, that of the Westerns and we do not know who we are. And when we speak Arabic, it is still in someone else's language that we speak, because by making Arabic the language of the Koran, God has stolen our language. He has made it unchangeable whereas man lives in time and needs to express himself a language, a tongue which evolves as rapidly as the spoken word" (47).

The relationship to politics takes on also a very different connotation for the political science student depending on his religion of reference. The university cannot take it into account in a country endangered by Moslem (48) and Jewish (49) fundamentalism and tempted by Christian conservatism (50).

16

For Islam, faith is a value in the political realm, or rather it is the only value in the political realm, the only one to give the political entity its raison d'être. The model of political life which refers to the times of the Prophet and the first Caliphes is the kingdom of God where the Koranic law is sufficient to guide the community of believers in its temporal activities and to orient it to the rewards of the next life (51). This theocracy can be compared to that which Israël knew at the time of Moses and the Judges. For Christianity on the other hand, by virtue of the gospel teachings themselves, the temporal and the spiritual realms are naturally distinct. Whatever may have been the accidental trappings taken on by Christianity, it was never identified with the Church.

One cannot deny this divergence of Christianity and Islan on the concept of society and the implication of this divergence in political science and legal studies. Many factors nevertheless do permit a fruitful dialogue on the themes, dialogue which has its place in the university. On the other hand, the divergences are not only of a theological nature: the differentiation between politics and religion in Christianity owes much to a thomist interpretation of Aristotle and to historical events which were first of all the emancipation from a pre-existing imperialist order; the non-differentiation for Islam owes much to neo-platonism and to historical events which were first of all the creation of an empire linked to a new faith (52). These differing viewpoints are now faced today with specific situations. Islam remains divided between a politico-religious unity of the Moslem community and the formation of ethnic and national units wherein is effected a desacralization of the economic and political conditions particularly when the citizens of that country are not all Moslems as is the case in Lebanon and Indonesia. On the contrary, the Christian principle of differentiation of politics and religion finds expression in a great diversity of ways, depending on the times and places (53). Finally Christianity and Islam are both confronted with modernity, that is a world which wants to be autonomous. They react to this claim, refusing, integrating or even claiming this autonomy depending on whether they see in it an insurmountable obstacle, a risk or an opportunity for faith (54). For a believer, this is the object of a fruitful dialogue.

2. HISTORICITY OF REVELATION AND UNIVERSITY TEACHING

No religion has given history the importance and the weight which Christianity has given it, whether one considers the importance given to irreversible events, whether one considers the progressive development of salvation, whether one considers the development of dogmas, whether one considers eschatology. That is why our universities of Christian inspiration should be expected to give more room to the teaching and research of history. I wish to recall here all that a knowledge of history can bring to the service of faith and more comprehensively to a better understanding between persons belonging to different cultures and religions.

What a knowledge of history brings to a Christian is first the revelation of God, God who reveals himself in and through history. One cannot but deplore, on this occasion, the laïcity of our Catholic universities in the latin tradition as opposed to those in the anglo-saxon tradition which make little provision in the curriculum from our religious history, beginning with the Bible. Vatican II has brought back the idea of a "people of God": There is no people if there is not history, if there is not memory. Our ancestors had understood this better than we when they were teaching religious history even to the illiterate by these illustrated stories which were the stained glass windows of our cathedrals. The roots of Christianity in history must be emphasized today more than ever, and therefore the necessity to teach that history. Without history and memory, the events of salvation would deteriorate into myths which each can reproduce according to his culture.

The knowledge of our religious history conveys also a certain picture of Christianity. That is why the way of grasping that history is important. It interprets and inculcates a way of thinking (mentality). The narrowness and partialty of national histories as taught to students has often been pointed out (55). The way the Church history is told does not avoid these shortcomings. It is less a distortion of events which studies can rectify in time, but rather a limited vision of reality due to the prejudices of a cultural, ideological or ecclesiological nature:

"History of the Church is written from a viewpoint where orthodoxy is priviledged as opposed to what, at certain moments, was not recognized as orthodox by the Church of that era... uniformity is priviledged over pluralism. The outcome is extremely serious in building doctrinal history and even spiritual history. Established Christianity is preferred over a changing Christianity... It is well known that the clergy aspect (clerical component) is given a priviledged place. That is why Church history has often been limited to a history of the clergy... There is moreover another abusive priviledge: the importance of the West over the Orient in all Church history written by Westerners. In addition though to a lesser degree, the favored position of the Oriental Greek Christianity over an Asiatic, African, Coptic Christianity... It is this behavior which explains the deep ignorance in our culture of the Christian experience as it was lived in other cultural or geographical areas..." (56).

There is no doubt that the profound changes of outlook which are taking place in the Christian world, and that the renewal of history so as to enlarge its traditional scope to that of other fields of human sciences (57) will accelerate an evolution which is already noticeable of the status of Church history (58). The Catholic Universities have an important role to play in this evolution.

Need it be to underscore that religious history when it is resituated, as it should, into a global history, opens up to a realistic view which makes an absolute only that which is truly so. The contribution of the historian to the hermaneutics of the ecclesiastical magisterium's declarations is to remind us of the historical nature of those declarations. Not only are these declarations brought about by a particular historical situation, to which the Church must face up, and these declarations run the risk of being distorted when applied to other situations, but also they are done in a particular cultural context. The wording used and the concept introduced are in fact determined by a historical intellectual situation that is by the mental structures of an era. "To say that Christian truth does not exist in an abstract state does not mean that it is encrusted with errors, but rather that it is molded in ideas and contingent schemes which determine its rational structure" (59). To bring forth, beyond the historical limitation, that which keeps a value for all times, is to bring history to play that role of catharsis which Henri Marrou attributed to it (60). This catharsis is necessary for a dialogue of cultures and even more so for a dialogue of religions.

3. UNIVERSALITY OF REVELATION AND UNIVERSITY TEACHING

The universal character of the Christian revelation has a different impact on teaching when it is confronted to diversities which are only cultural and when it is confronted with divergent religious convictions.

The requirements of a universality of Christian revelation which respects cultural differences and which implies a pluralism in the expression of a same faith meet no opposition in principle and present no insoluble problems as long as the same faith is concerned. A university of Christian inspiration is not with means in its teaching to defuse narrow-minded views and to receive cultural diversities (61). Although the respect of differences should not turn into a radicalization of these differences. The integration of differences is a condition of catholicity; in a broader sense, it is a requirement of the human mind:

"The capacity to integrate differences is a basic requirement of human reasoning: that is to open up to the universal which is necessary to the development of the personality. It points to acculturation as a collective and individual necessity. The multiplying of contacts between cultures which characterizes our times is therefore that which forces man to implement cultural possibilities hitherto unexploited... That acculturation is a necessary condition does not suffice to make it successful... The intercultural relations must be the object of conscious arrangements, based on an exact appreciation of those two fundamental notions which are cultural relativism and development" (62).

The cultural relativism does not mean that one puts all cultures on the same level and at all periods of history. Is this not the meaning of a statement of John Paul II, which is quoted at times out of its context: "There are new points, perspectives, philosophical languages which are undoubtedly deficient; there are scientific systems so limited, so narrow, that they make it impossible to express and interpret in a satisfactory way the Word of God" (63).

With regard to development, it is clear that in a university of Christian inspiration, it cannot be measured in terms of economic growth, but rather in the quality of life. As John Paul II declared: "The Catholic university must show... how an authentic faith, solid and dynamic, is capable of evaluating positively the cultures it approaches, to receive those human values which may be brought to Christ and even to bring about new cultures which give specific expression to the human aspects which are included in Christianity" (64). This does not therefore imply that modern culture can be taken on without discernment (65).

Cultural pluralism should not therefore present insoluble problems to university teaching. It only needs an acknowledgment of similarities and differences. The plurality of religions does bring up a more difficult problem, not that there are not similarities among religions nor that these should not be enhanced; Vatican II has in fact done it for Islam (66). But because it is often what we call the difference which gives a religion its internal cohesion. For example, can we ignore incarnation when speaking of Christianity, or can Christians recognize themselves in the "People of the Book", whatever may be the respect this expression receives from the Moslems? The Director of the Institute of Islamic-Christian Studies of our university wrote appropriately:

"To grasp the original meaning of a religion, one must penetrate to its nucleus, its heart, which give to the constituting elements their structure and internal relationships... If therefore there appears to be a convergence between the perspectives and concepts of God, of man and of the world, which corresponds to both religions, fundamentally what is perceived and underscored is the difference. Now this difference cannot be left aside, otherwise one falls into syncretism which ignores the originality and specificity of each. This difference must, on the contrary, be maintained by respect for truth and for the preservation of authenticity. And it is by beginning with this difference that one can envisage a true and authentic collaboration" (67).

The acceptance of pluralism is even in the field of religions the acceptance of the difference. In the case of religions like Christianity and Islam which purport to be universal in their conception of the world one may evidently ask if the attitude is not contradictory. Karl Rahner believed this was not do for Christianity. Even a thoroughly universal conception of the world mut become aware of its historical evolution. It has a point of departure inevitably very specific. There is a difference between on the one hand what it is aiming at and which has not yet the full blossoming of experience, and on the other, the particular historical image which for the time being it often achieves. Moreover it is on condition one recognizes this historicity which assumes a future reality that a world conception can anticipate and justify this universality. If therefore it is open to the future, a religion must dialogue with other religions to enrich its own reflection on the historical experience of others. Truth is not made relative if one considers incomplete one's own grasp of truth (68).

+ + +

In order to analyze the cultural status of revelation and its taking into account in a university teaching where there is cultural pluralism, we have chosen the three themes of transcendance, historicity and universality. These are three characteristics of Christian revelation which cannot be dissociated but not always easy to reconcile. Thus, and principally in the light of the problem of modernity, should appear the question of the relationship between faith, religions, and cultures, and the correlated relation of the Church-Society, directed in turn by the Church-Kingdom of God relation... A real dialogue in a pluricultural and pluri-religious society depends in effect upon the answer to these questions. It is by establishing, if not a dissociation, at least a clear distinction between faith and religion and a partial identification of religion and culture (69) that one may hold religion in a relative perspective, not identify it to an absolute, to fully given truth and thus to leave an open door to history and dialogue. That dialogue we shall refer to it only at its two extreme points, the building of a social reality, the building of the spiritual dimension of a person.

The first level of dialogue is not that which Harvey Cox would bring forth in reference to the "Church of the Secular University": "Christian and Arabic scholars seem to have gotten along perfectly well as soon as they forgot their debates on the Holy Trinity and the One God Allah, and that they started dissecting animals, and probing the skies through telescopes" (70). It is not at this non religious level that Vatican II makes reference when it encourages the faithful of all religions to "work together, without violence and deceit, in order to build up the world in genuine peace"; this exhortation is in fact preceeded by a rationale: "Therefore if we have been summoned to the same destiny which is both human and divine, we can and we should work together..." (71). The dialogue referred to is religious because a fundamental dimension of the dialogue of religions among themselves is the dialogue of religions with the world. This rejects the idea of a Christian or a Moslem Society, which would be a preexisting archetype, which obliterates history and any dialogue. This also rejects an atheistic society refusing all spiritual outlook. The Church if it does not pretend to be the keystone of society, does not see itself fitting into the atheistic society and recognizes that other religions have a capital role to play namely to provide meaning and to mould consciences. It is a dialogue which is not independent of respective beliefs but because of them.

At the other end of the spectrum is that type of dialogue which Raimundo Panikkar has called "intra-religious": "One does not dialogue only with one own tradition or with others as such but rather with one's own self having assimilated in one's own way a conception of reality which has drawn from different sources... When I will have discovered the atheist in me, the Hindu and the Christian in me, when I will look upon my brother as another me, and when the other will not feel alienated in me, then we shall be approaching the Kingdom" (72). Raimundo Panikkar prefers an interior dialogue committing faith, hope and charity and being the meeting of two religions in the heart of a believer rather than inter-religious dialogues which in anthropology, sociology or theology (we shall not refer to them here) put in opposition, in a courteous and profitable way, repre-sentatives of various religions. If religions are many, the religious experience is one.

This intrareligious dialogue could just as well describe the itinerary of a Louis Massignon who has been deeply influenced by the religious experience of Al-Hallaj (73). In the case of Islam, it is very signi-ficant that it is at the level of mystics, usually referred to as soufis that this intrareligious dialogue takes place. It is perhaps thus because the soufis, who are considered suspicious by sunnite Islam, "have challenged the God of the Law and reintroduced religious conscience in the movement of history" (74). The expe-rience of mystics has a universal value and raises a religion to the level of a true quest of the Absolute. It is in the mystics that are fully reconciled the transcendance, the historicity and the universality of the revelation.

+ + + + +

NOTES

(1) Vatican II, <u>Dogmatic Constitution on Divine Revelation</u> n° 2. quoting Eph. 1,9 and 2,18.

(2) Gen. 12,1

(3) Is. 43, 15

(4) II Cor. 5, 17

(5) Gal. 6, 15

(6) Jn. 1, 13

(7) Ap. 21, 5

(8) Epist. 14 (Patr. Gr. 46, 1052 C)

(9) <u>Confessions</u>, trad. J. TRABUCCO, Garnier-Flammarion 1964, p. 54.

(10) Henri de LUBAC, <u>La foi chrétienne</u>, Aubier 1969 "Les solécismes chrétiens" pp. 255-283.

(11) Henri BOUILLARD, <u>Comprendre ce que l'on croit</u>. Aubier 1971, p. 120.

(12) Gabriel WIDMER, Théologie et Philosophie, dans <u>Revue de Théologie et de Philosophie</u>, 1968 p. 375.

(13) I Cor. 11, 1.

(14) <u>Epître à Diognète</u>, trad. H. MARROU; Coll. Sources chrétiennes. Le Cerf, 1965.

(15) Mt. 5, 48.

(16) Ph. 3, 8.

(17) Jean AUCAGNE, L'Islam par rapport à l'unicité et à la division du peuple de Dieu, dans <u>L'Unique Israël de Dieu</u>, sous la direction de Jean-Michel GARRIGUES, Criterion 1987, p. 198. To this doctrinal element may be added a historical one: Judaism in Medina and Christianity in Byzantium seemed to the religions of two enemy peoples; the Arabs wanted also to have their own religion, preached by a prophet coming from among them (ibid. p. 203).

(18) <u>Théologie et choc des cultures</u>, Le Cerf 1984, p.183.

(19) <u>Exhortation apostolique Catechesi tradendae</u>, October 16, 1979 (Oss. Rom. November 2, 1979 and Doc. Cath. n° 1773, p. 914).

(20) HANS KUNG, <u>Le Christianisme et les religions du monde</u>, Le Seuil 1986, pp. 176-187.

(21) Jean DANIELOU, Aux origines de l'Eglise. Christianisme, Judaisme, Hellénisme, dans la revue <u>AXES</u>, Tome XII, 1-2-3. 1979-1980, p. 101.

(22) Oscar CULLMANN, Christologie du Nouveau Testament, Delachaux et Niestlé, 1958, p. 283.

(23) Henri de LUBAC, Petit catéchisme sur nature et grâce, Fayard, 1980, p. 50. To assimilate without being assimilated, this was also the attitude of Islam with regard to Greek culture; see also Gustave VON GRUNEBAUM, Islam and Medieval Hellenism, London, 1976 and Vincenzo POGGI, L'Inculturation au début de l'Islam, Inculturation VI, Rome, 1984.

(24) Vatican II, Pastoral Constitution on the Church in the Modern World, n° 58. On the ecclesiology in the post-conciliar period, with its tendencies to be more open or to withdraw onto oneself, three books may be consulted:
- La réception de Vatican II sous la direction d'ALBERIGO et JOSUA, Le Cerf, 1985.
- Vingt ans après Vatican II, Synode extraordinaire, Le Centurion, 1986.
- Le retour des certitudes (Evénements et orthodoxie depuis Vatican II) sous la direction de Paul LADRIERE et René LUVEAU, Le Centurion, 1987.

(25) The book by Paul VALADIER, L'Eglise en procès (catholicisme et société moderne), Calman-Lévy, 1987, is an excellent reflection on the evolution of contemporary society and how Catholicism may situate itself in the future.

(26) Inculturation has been dealt with in many writings. We offer two references providing an overview: Bruno CHENU, Théologies chrétiennes des tiers-mondes (latino-américaine, noire américaine, noire sud-africaine, asiatique), Le Centurion, 1987, and Deane William FERM, Third World Liberation Theologies, MARYKNOLL, Orbis Books 1986. For each region one may consult:

- In Africa, Aylward SHORTER, Théologie chrétienne africaine, Le Cerf, 1980 and René LUNEAU, Laisse aller mon peuple, Karthala, 1987, and two pontifical documents, Africae Terrarum, Paul VI's message to Africa, Oss. Rom. 1° nov. 1967 and Doc. Cath. 19 nov. 1967, and La théologie africaine, address by John Paul II to Bishops in Zaïre, Oss. Rom. May 1, 1983 and Doc. Cath. June 19, 1983.

- In Asia, two brochures: La politique de l'Inculturation en Asie Orientale, Pro Mundi Vitae, n° 104, Brussels, 1986, and Building the Church in Pluricultural Asia, Inculturation VII, Rome, 1986,

and the Reports of the Federation of Bishops' Conferences in Asia (F.A.B.C. Papers).

- In Latin America and on Liberation Theology,
Gustavo GUTIERREZ, Théologie de la libération,
Brussels, Lumen Vitae, 1974, as a basis reference,
to be completed by Marcello AZEVEDO, Communautés
ecclésiales de base, Centurion, 1986. The main
texts about this controverse will be found in
Théologie de la libération, Documents et débats,
Cerf/Centurion, 1985, and in two Instructions by
the Congregation for the Doctrine of Faith, witnesses
of the evolution of appraisal: Aspects de la
théologie de la libération, Doc. Cath. 1984 n°
1881, and la liberté chrétienne et la libération,
Doc. Cath. April 20, 1986, n°1916; and in John
Paul II's letter to the Bishops of Brazil on April
9, 1986, Doc. Cath. June 1°, 1986 n° 1919.

(27) Walter KASPER, Dogme et Evangile, Casterman 1967
p. 27.
(28) Unité de la foi et pluralisme théologique, session
of October 1972 of the International Commission
of Theology, Doc. Cath. May 20, 1973, n° 1632,
pp. 459-460.
(29) Hervé-Marie LEGRAND, Inverser Babel, Mission de
l'Eglise, dans Spiritus n° 43, Paris 1970 and Henri
de LUBAC, Les Eglises particulières dans l'Eglise
universelle, Aubier, 1971.

(30) Vatican II, Decree on the Church's Missionary
Activity, n° 22.
(31) Jean AUCAGNE, Inculturation arabe au Liban, théories
et réalités, in AXES, April 1982.
(32) Cf. Aloysius PIERIS, L'Asie non sémitique face
aux modèles occidentaux d'inculturation, et Bruno
CHENU, Glissements progressifs d'un agir mission-
naire, dans Lumière et Vie, July 1984.
(33) Vatican II, Dogmatic Constitution on the Church,
n° 14, 15 and 16.
(34) Vatican II, Declaration on the Relationships of
the Church to non Christian Religions, n° 2, 3
and 4.
(35) Vatican II, Pastoral Constitution on the Church
in the Modern World, n° 22.
(36) Joseph MOINGT, Rencontre des religions, in Etudes,
January 1987.

(37) On the evolution of the Christian theology of religions and the problems raised, one may consult Paul F. KNITTER, No other Name? A Critical Survey of Christian Attitudes Toward the World Religions, Maryknoll, Orbis Books, 1985, and the article by Claude GEFFRE, La théologie des religions non-chrétiennes vingt ans après Vatican II, in Islamo-christiana, n° 11, 1985.

(38) Joseph MOINGT, Religion du salut et salut en Jésus-Christ, report made in Beirut on February 8, 1985, typed draft.

(39) Michel SALES, Le Christianisme, la culture et les cultures, in AXES, January 1981.

(40) Cf. Edouard BONÉ, l'Université Catholique, une difficile vocation, in ETUDES, April 1988. It is not without interest to contrast the chapter on university by Harvey COX, twenty years ago, in "L'Eglise de l'Université Séculière" in The Secular City, Casterman, 1968.

(41) See the thematic report of the 12th General Assembly of the IFCU: The Catholic University, Instrument of Cultural Pluralism in the Service of the Church and Society, August 1978.

(42) Report, pp. 64-77.

(43) Vatican II, Pastoral Constitution on the Church in the Modern World, n° 36. In the book of Genesis, God asks man to give a name to all creatures and it is even man who gives woman her name (Gen. 2, 19-23). In the Koran, it is God who teaches man the name of all beings and reminds man that He alone has this power which even Angels cannot have (Koran, 2nd sourate 31-32).

(44) Ibid. n° 43. The role of conscience is often recalled in Vatican II. Islam recognizes with difficulty this form of mediation. Joseph VAN ESS writes appropriately "a moslem does not act according to his conscience but in accordance with the will of God" (in Hans KUNG, op. cit. p. 76). This does not imply that Moslems have a lesser sense of morality than Christians. But the importance of the law is such in arabic-moslem culture that the law dispenses one from referring to morality.

(45) See for example, Michel FALISE: Une pratique chrétienne de l'économie, Le Centurion, 1985; Mgr. Gabriel MATAGRIN: Politique, Eglise et Foi, Pour une pratique chrétienne de la politique, Le

Centurion, 1972; André BARRAL-BARON: Comprendre
nos différences, Chemins du discernement humain,
Le Centurion, 1984.

(46) Michel ALLARD, Aux étudiants en langue et littérature
arabes, in Travaux et Jours, December 1977, p.11.
See also Michel HAYEK, L'originalité de l'apport
chrétien dans les lettres arabes, in Normes et
Valeurs de l'Islam contemporain, Payot, 1966, pp.
115-131.

(47) Paul NWYIA, l'Islam face à la crise du langage
moderne, in Travaux et Jours, January 1971, p.101.

(48) Bruno ETIENNE, L'Islam radical, Hachette, 1987,
and Amir TAHERI, La terreur sacrée, Sylvie Messinger,
1987.

(49) In his book The Decadence of Judaïsm in our Time,
New York, Exposition Press, 1965, Moshe MENUHIM
has very well shown how the identification of Judaïsm
and Zionism could only but change the spirituality
and universality of Judaïsm. But is Zionism not
the result of Antisemitism? And the appeal of Zionism
which is quite different from country to country
is it not dependent on the ability of each country
to integrate citizens while respecting their ethnic
and religious features?

(50) The "specificity" of the political realities is
ignored by the Catholic realm and the Moslem as
well. "In past times, the union between Church
and Catholic State produced a Catholic realm, perfect
implementation of the social kingship of our Lord
Jesus Christ" (Mgr. Lefebvre, Ils l'ont découronné,
Fideliter, 1987, p. 211).

(51) Louis GARDET, La Cité musulmane, Vrin, 1954.

(52) Bertrand BADIE, Les deux Etats. Pouvoir et société
en Occident et en Terre d'Islam, Fayard, 1987.

(53) Jean-Claude ESLIN, Three types of separation of
religion and politics are described in ESPRIT,
April-May, 1986.

(54) For Christianism, see, for example, Paul VALADIER,
L'Eglise en procès, Catholicisme et société moderne,
Calmann-Lévy, 1987, et Marcel GAUCHET, Le désenchan-
tement du monde, une histoire politique de la
religion, Gallimard, 1985. For Islam, see Daryush
CHAYEGAN, Qu'est-ce qu'une révolution religieuse,
Presse d'aujourd'hui, Paris, 1982, et L'Islam et
la Modernité, dans Familles musulmanes et Modernité,
Publisud, 1986.

(55) Suzanne CITRON, <u>Enseigner l'Histoire aujourd'hui</u>, Editions ouvrières, 1984.

(56) Giuseppe ALBERIGO, Nouvelles frontières de l'histoire de l'Eglise, in <u>CONCILIUM</u>, 1970, n°57 p.61.

(57) cf. Jacques LE GOFF, "L'histoire nouvelle" dans <u>La nouvelle histoire</u>, Retz, 1978.

(58) To measure transformations which religious history has confirmed, see: <u>Introduction aux sciences humaines des religions</u>, symposium gathered by H. DESROCHE and J. SEGUY, Cujas, 1970, and Dominique JULIA, La religion - Histoire religieuse, in <u>Faire de l'Histoire</u>, Gallimard, 1974, T. 2.

(59) Roger AUBERT, L'Histoire de l'Eglise, une clé indispensable à l'interprétation des décisions du magistère, in <u>CONCILIUM</u>, 1970, n°57, p. 91, and the article of Yves CONGAR, L'histoire de l'Eglise, lieu théologique.

(60) Henri MARROU, <u>De la connaissance historique</u>, Le Seuil, 1954, p. 273.

(61) One might consult, given the lack of research on cultural diversity in the programs of higher education, the OCDE study, <u>L'Education multiculturelle</u>, Paris, 1987, and the article by Michel de CERTEAU, Pour une Ecole de la diversité, pp. 170-203. On the epistemology and methodology of intercultural dialogue, see Martine ABDALLAH PRETCEILLE, <u>Vers une pédagogie interculturelle</u>, La Sorbonne, 1986.

(62) Sélim ABOU, <u>L'identité culturelle</u>, Anthropos, 1986, preface to the 2nd edition, p. XIV.

(63) <u>Discours à l'Université Grégorienne</u>, Doc. Cath. February 3, 1980, n°1779.

(64) <u>Discours aux Professeurs de l'Université de Milan</u>, Doc. Cath. July 3, 1983, n°1855.

(65) cf. Gérard DEFOIS, Etre moderne, une fatalité? in <u>ETUDES</u>, January 1987.

(66) Vatican II, <u>Declaration on the Relationship of the Church to non Christian Religions</u>, n°3.

(67) Augustin DUPRE LA TOUR, "L'Institut d'études islamo-chrétiennes de Beyrouth", in <u>Lumen Vitae</u>, 1980, n°4, p.487.

(68) Karl RAHNER, "Sur le dialogue dans la société pluraliste", in <u>Ecrits théologiques</u>, t. VII, Paris, 1967, pp. 23-36. We shall not deal with the matter of "anonymous Christians"; see Bernard SESBOUE, "Karl Rahner et les chrétiens anonymes", ETUDES,

November 1984, pp. 521-535, and Karl RAHNER, "Jésus-Christ dans les religions non chrétiennes" in Traité fondamental de la Foi, Le Centurion, 1983, pp. 348-359.

(69) Paul TILLICH, Théologie de la culture, Edit. Planète, 1968, and Dietrich BONHOEFFER, Résistance et soumission, Geneva, 1963, have elucidated these distinctions.
(70) Harvey COX, La Cité séculière, Casterman, 1968, p. 239.
(71) Vatican II, Pastoral Constitution on the Church in the Modern World, n° 92.
(72) Raimundo PANIKKAR, Le dialogue intrareligieux, Aubier, 1985, pp. 9 et 12. Those who might be concerned about Raimundo Panikkar's itinerary "When I left, I was Christian, I found myself to be a hindu and I returned being a buddhist without having ceased to be a Christian" (p. 50), I suggest to read Yves RAGUIN, L'Esprit sur le monde, Desclée de Brouwer, 1987, coll. Christus n°40: "The missionnary must try to go along with other religions... His spirituality will be enriched not by the left-overs of other religions but by the rediscovery of Christ" (p.147).

(73) Louis MASSIGNON, Akhbar Al-Hallaj, French translation, Paris, 1936 and Diwan d'Al-Hallaj, French translation, Geuthner, 1955.
(74) Paul NWYIA, Exégèse coranique et langage mystique, Beirut, 1970, p. 8.

+ + + + +

Cultural diversity in the university
and our commitment within the cultural reality of society

by Msgr. Gérard DEFOIS
Rector of the Catholic University
Lyons, France

At Lyons, we are familiar with the first type of situation as described by Father Ducruet in his proposals of 1 March 1986: "those cultures which have been markedly Christian in faith for a long time, which have seen their Christian values pushed aside or even contradicted in favour of a variety of factors, particularly the technico-scientific mentality, and a new culture, sometimes called secular or modern; such cultures have developed especially in the Europe-America area".

First, some figures: in our university about 15% of the youth or adults come from foreign countries, with some 70 different nationalities. There is a large number first of all at the French Language and Cultural Institute -- they come to learn our language -- then in the social sciences and in theology. Most of them come from the Third World, particularly Africa. They are seeking Western culture, among other things management techniques, sociology and reflection on the development of peoples. But, if at first there is a desire to conform to our schemes of action and socialization through production, soon afterwards conflict arises between their own heritage and the new knowledge. A cultural shock takes place between tradition and European innovation.

A survey made at the time of the Pope's visit revealed, among members of the student body who responded, the following: 55% practising Catholics, 6% non-Catholic Christians, 3% non-Christian but with a religious faith; and 36% non-practising, non-believing and indifferent.

Beyond this brief picture, it seems to me that the cultural diversity in which we live is first of all that of the European society before being specifically that of the Catholic university. We are in fact experiencing what Father Ducruet has observed: "the laicism of our Catholic universities of Latin tradition which, contrary to those in the Anglo-Saxon tradition, offer little space in their programme for our religious history, starting with the Bible." (1) This is not simply the result of negligence on the part of teachers, which could be remedied through pedagogical means; it is the academic translation of a moral and intellectual evolution -- basic protests which, since the era of the Enlightenment have marginalized religion into the sphere of privacy and intimacy and reduced it to the barest requirements of the private individual and strictly confessional beliefs. French education has been experiencing this cultural conflict from within itself for at least two centuries John Paul II, when receiving the European bishops, mentioned in this respect in 1982: "If, during successive crises, European culture has sought to distance itself from the Faith and the Church, what was then proclaimed as a desire for emancipation and autonomy was, in reality, an interior crisis of the European conscience itself, sorely tried and tempted in its most basic identity, in its fundamental choices and its historic destiny." (2)

Man's drama of symbols and convictions, practices and references goes beyond the simple statement of differences that respect for pluralism or a peaceful dialogue would suffice to bring together. We are in fact at the heart of a confrontation of cultures, between the Judeo-Christian tradition and the scientific or technical programmes which have generated our economic growth or our social development against a background which is by turns either Marxist ideology or liberal philosophy. What these two have in common is a refusal of transcendence and the Promethean vision of man. If there is indeed a protest from the clerical and religious authorities, we must of course see that it originated ahead of such matters as the functioning of institutions or communication among differing attitudes.

But one would still be blinded by remaining at the level of polemics between the old and the new, the conservatives and the partisans of change, men of tradition and militants for progress. However media-oriented it might be, this basic Manicheism obscures the radical problem of our societies: how, in the state of modernity and technical progress -- which is the basis of education in our Catholic universities --, can we satisfy the search for cultural identity, permanence and security which is expressed by French students as well as by students from other contries? Secularization, criticism and the valorization of change are written into our programmes, they loosen the ties of memory and customs which form cultural identity. It has often been said, and Father Ducruet reminded us of it: "without history and memory, the incidents of salvation would degenerate into myth." (3) The constraints of technical training have flattened the cultivation of the Judeo-Christian heritage in people's mind. To the point where we have the impression of facing young people without a past, they are so ignorant and illiterate on the subject of philosophy and theology. It is because science and technological progress have been set up as the ultimate criteria for truth, while tradition, the revelation of the history of man in God seems marginal to them. Thus, Christianity is relegated **culturally** -- I insist on the word -- to the limited field of the emotional and the useless, as a personal belief without serious significance; it is in the nature of an obscurantist myth and thus outmoded in a rational society.

Here, students from abroad show reluctance; they protest in the name of their roots, unless they have thrown themselves entirely into the Western technologies up to the point of losing their soul and their memory. For this progress promises possessions and power. It is evident that this tension, this cultural drama is the field of action of a Catholic university. The university itself wants to remain true to itself both in welcoming widely and in maintaining its spiritual identity; it must be a place of professional guidance integrating young people into the production society; it prepares them for the technical organization of the economy and of international exchanges. Which means that it involves its students in the dynamic movement of modernization which has become a global project of world development. But it remains Catholic in its vision of man, its memory and the hope of salvation through Jesus Christ.

The question of the specificity of our universities is indeed the fruit of this discussion today. We are involved in the cultural reality of society through this crisis of social consensus. It is normal that students experience this crisis. It calls forth from us a creative will to give meaning to modernity within the Christian tradition.

One must not, I think, be taken in by present-day allegations that all this is first of all a question of authority. Thus, I do not think that Rome, for example, would be conservative on the subject of personal morality and daring in regard to social matters. I perceive in the positions taken by the magisterium the same conceptual attitude operating in the two realms (4). What is involved is man's specific relationship to nature, to the body, to history and to moral philosophy. What is at stake is our cultural differences within society: between nature as received creation and the technology of exploitation, between the body as endless desire and the human being doomed to die or to err, between history as production and time as escatological calling, between ethics as an absolute norm and competition as the autonomous regulation of interests. If cultural conflict drifts into Manicheism, it will be distorted by mythological struggles, either in basic and emotional terms or in relation to political forces. In such instances, our universities will have failed in their task of a specific cultural creation.

These rapid thoughts show how our Catholic universities in Latin countries are at the heart of Christian action toward modernity. For us who train engineers, biologists, computer experts, community developers, and above all theologians, we find ourselves right in the middle of the argument of tradition versus progress. This cultural confrontation exists within young people themselves; in their uncertainty, many are again looking for signs and points of reference. Young Israelis recently reproached their parents: "You did not know how to make us love the roots of our identity". (5) This appeal is also addressed to us in France. Students suspect our uncertainty and our doubts, our questioning and our excessive openmindedness. And it is not always an easy question to deal with. But is is also an appeal to rediscover, with regard to modernity or to the technology of our societies, a new creative liberty.

It would be naive to think that this situation is new. These tensions have been woven into the European conscience since the Middle Ages. Nevertheless the modern scientific and technological culture has thrust itself, like a monopoly, on the entire world and with it has come a certain view of things and of man. For us, to rediscover memory and intelligence is, under these conditions, the challenge of a new Christian humanism. The future of culture is the task of our universities.

(1) Report of Father Ducruet: "Christian faith in the context of cultural pluralism", p. 18

(2) Osservatore Romano of 7 October 1982

(3) Report of Father Ducruet, p. 187

(4) Gérard Defois, To be modern, is it inevitable ?
Etudes, January 1987

(5) Y. Rash: Israel, a puzzled youth, Etudes, May 1988,
p. 592

A brief response to Jean Ducruet's paper:
"Christian Faith in a Situation of Cultural Pluralism"

by Kevin G. O'CONNELL, S.J.
President, Le Moyne College
Syracuse, New York, USA

I am a last-minute replacement on this panel, since I was asked only yesterday afternoon. Moreover, in a panel whose other members have prepared short presentations on specific topics, I represent an aspect of cultural pluralism, because I was asked to make some reflections on Father Ducruet's paper which I saw for the first time only yesterday.

It is a closely written paper with two main parts, the first on the cultural status of revelation (and by this he means Christian revelation), the second on that status in relation to university teaching. While the second part has many interesting observations, especially in its first section on transcendance (where he discusses helpfully several difficulties for the acquisition of knowledge and the formation of consciences to discernment that arise in the cultural context of a Christian university in Lebanon), I will use my limited time today to make some comments on the three sections of Part One.

I take this first half of the paper to be an originally unified presentation in itself, a sort of a "white paper" on the topic, the cultural status of revelation. In it, Father Ducruet discusses successively three features or aspects of revelation in relation to human cultures. They are transcendance, historicity, and universality. At the end of Part One, he reminds us quite properly that these features, though viewed separately, are really inseparable and must be kept together.

In discussing the transcendance of revelation and human cultures, Father Ducruet stresses the absolute character of revelation as a call to <u>leave behind</u> one's culture and to set out for the new and as-yet non-cultural. He cites the call of Abram in Genesis to leave the culture of Sumer and Akhad, as well as Paul's call to the early Christians at Corinth to leave behind their old cultural ways (their gods, customs, perhaps even modes of thought). Moreover, he sees the statement at the end of the Apocalypse "Behold, I make all things new" (to which I would compare the statement in Second Isaiah about forgetting what has been done by God in the past, since God's new actions of deliverance from exile in Babylon will outshine even the past acts of deliverance in the exodus from Egypt) - he sees that statement as an excellent expression of "the gratuitous character of Christian Revelation... It does not stem from any human culture; it is not the blossoming of any human culture; it is commensurate with no human culture. This cultural inadequacy can be felt at all levels, that of language, that of concepts, that of behaviour."

While, at least in part, this point is meant to highlight the contrast between Christianity (as transcending culture) and Islam (with its particular - and unchanging - language and its general cultural rootedness), I think it is overstated. Islam, some forms of Judaism, and certainly various major strains within Christianity (such as Eastern Orthodoxy or pre-Vatican II Roman Catholicism) all try repeatedly to freeze the cultural movement at a certain favored (and familiar) moment and to make that moment definitive for all time. Islam's sacralization of Arabic is surely matched by the place of Latin within Roman Catholicism for many centuries until the changes introduced by Vatican II. It is not an accident that Islam recognizes an affinity in Judaism and Christianity by calling them religions of the Book.

However, living culture is always changing (even if not perceived so by its adherents), and these changes are a vehicle for revelation, too. This is true not only for Judaism and Christianity, but even for Islam, which has more than one branch and which is changing before our eyes today in Iran and the Mideast (not least under the pressure of those fundamentalists who are attempting to restore what they understand as an ideal - or the only valid - form of Islam).

I guess what I am suggesting is that the concept of transcendance is itself a cultural concept that has a value within our Christian culture (and in some other cultures), but it can no longer be absolutized in our thought. Early Christianity, for example, was at odds with (and transcended) its surrounding culture precisely because it arose in a period of intense cultural change.

In his section on the historicity of revelation and human cultures, Father Ducruet dismisses the view (accepted, he says, by Küng among others) that early Judeo-Christianity has disappeared into the Christian Hellenistic Church, and he stresses the importance of Hellenism for the development of Christianity. While I certainly agree with his main point, that one cannot simply "peel away" the cultural development induced in early Christianity by Hellenism and thereby recover some sort of original or pristine Christianity that would be authoritative for present-day Christianity, I think that his argument would be strengthened by the perspective of Hegel (in his massive Judentum und Hellenismus) and of others that Hellenism was a vital force shaping Jewish life and culture (and therefore faith) already in the third and second centuries before Christ. The conflicts between types of Judaism (due to such "outside" influences as Hellenism, as well as Iranian religion) find their echoes within early Christianity.

Moreover, what happened in early Christianity (analogous to what had happened earlier in Israelite religion as, for example, the Davidic monarchy and its implications changed the meaning and force of covenant) continued to happen in the development of both Eastern and Western Christianity. New and diverse cultural influences repeatedly changed the self-understanding and expression of Christianity in the past - sometimes boiling up in conflict (and perhaps giving rise to a dogmatic definition), sometimes finding relatively easy acceptance by most or all (one thinks especially of the major changes in Christianity due to its public acceptance in the Roman Empire under Constantine).

Change or development reshapes a living tradition but doesn't need to be seen as breaking that tradition. To accept flexibility, to live flexibly within change, is a choice - and so is rejection of flexibility, rigidity of life, and rejection of change - and that choice divides people of our time, even Christian people, even Catholic faithful and Catholic thinkers, just as it has in the past and as it will, I am sure, in the future. It cannot escape any of us that the dispute with Archbishop Lefebvre is about just such a choice.

I am particularly appreciative of Father Ducruet's discussion of the universality of revelation and human cultures in the third section of Part One. He notes quite rightly that Vatican II has been an important event (even a "cultural factor") for Catholic life.

We now understand better that respect for cultural differences and a pluralism in the expression of the same faith are required by universalism. We may not always want to admit that this new understanding is a fruit of culture, probably Western European and North American cultures (with their experiences of pluralism), and not all within our religious tradition find this cultural development welcome. Archbishop Lefebvre is not the only one who is put off and disaffected by a development that seems hostile to what he perceived as the life of Catholicism.

Anyway, the shift in understanding has happened, and cultural forces will interact rather vigorously for some time to come.

From our contemporary perspective, we can perhaps see that at least some old sources of division within Christianity were not demanded by faith, or that they need not be maintained any longer. Perhaps, too, some of the issues that divide us within the contemporary Church will seem equally peripheral and unfortunate to those who come after us. (I think especially of questions about ordained ministry for women and married men, about the structure of papal governance in relation to bishops, or about pluralism as legitimate within theological education). In any event, we have to wrestle with our own time and our own experiences. And we need to do this in ways that allow freedom of expression (and freedom to develop differently) to particular local churches as active partners within the universal Church.

Since my time is up, and our chairman is eying me anxiously, I will stop here.

Later, in response to a question, I added: "It is as important for the North American Church as it is for the Philippine Church or for any other particular local Church to receive active support and encouragement from Rome, rather than warnings and suspicion, as we each engage in our own struggle to be Catholic in ways appropriate to our cultural context."

+ + + + +

FAITH AND CULTURE:

A CHALLENGE TO UNIVERSITIES IN LATIN AMERICA

by Rev. Julio Teran Dutari
Rector of P.U.C. of Ecuador

The subject of this report follows the line of the Puebla Document and brings us to the first ecclesiastical events of Santo Domingo, on the fifth centenary of the American evangelization. It is valid for everything touching the historic relationship between faith and culture on our continent (I am considering here mainly Spanish America, but I believe I could also include a good portion of the Portuguese-speaking territories); this is valid moreover for everything which involves the role that the university is called upon to play in this relationship.

In the first part, I will present a diachronic vision of the cultural evolution, demonstrating some important signs of the presence of faith, in three stages or levels; there will also appear a culturally pluralistic panorama in which tensions and conflicts are produced, but with a constantly renewed creativity for continually seeking new syntheses. In the second part, I will try to formulate concrete tasks which present themselves to the Catholic university, given the present situation of faith as it faces cultural problems.

1. CULTURAL EVOLUTION AND THE POSITION FAITH ASSUMES

Although it would be unjust to speak of just one Latin-American culture and even of a homogeneous evolution of cultures in Latin America, nevertheless one can establish levels of the cultural problem common to all our countries, especially with regard to the situation of faith. These levels are superposed in different cultural regions in various ways and at coinciding moments in history; but in general, one can appreciate in all of this a dynamic integration of pluralistic cultural forms, marked precisely by those deep forces which have a lot to do with the Christian faith.

1.1. Formation of a mixed cultural matrix

From the sixteenth century to the present day, a process of cross-breeding, not only racial, but also specifically cultural, has developed on a large scale and has formed a new historic unity with its own creative characteristics. It was a case of the fertile meeting between the Iberian culture (the "masculine" element) and the indigenous cultures (the "feminine" element). In the two elements there was a dominating religious factor: from the Iberian side, the Catholic faith, for a long time part of the culture in this extreme south-western part of Europe and carried here to America at a moment of extraordinary strength for its cultural influence; from the indigenous side came the intense and unifying religiosity of a vision of the cosmos and of a feeling for life.

In the beginning, there was a dramatic meeting in the clash of cultures, whose meaning - not only theoretical or simply as pretext, but also effective and constructive - was evangelization (understood naturally in a manner a little distinct from that of the post-conciliar theology of today). But there came out of this a veritable synthesis, not always justified as such by our intellectuals (historians, sociologists, philosophers and theologians who are opposed to the significance of the fifth centenary...), even when it remains in any case an undeniable fact, especially when observed from the outside, as from the magnificent vantage point of this Southeast Asian continent where we meet today. To any regard free of prejudice can only appear the collective physionomy of the Latinamerican who is culturally no longer either European or indigenous, but has become someone new, born from these two parents in the anguish of childbirth.

There is a common background of values on which are shaped different nationalities, with all their elements of culture: in the religious sphere, which has the deepest roots, this appears as a popular Catholic religiosity; in the political sphere, as a special form of Christianity which had its origins in royal protection under the Hispanic empire and which, even afterwards, retained a common reference - with a different but substantial symbol - in the way of bringing together Church and State; in other cultural spheres, such as the proper structures of family, education, work, festival, local community, link to homeland, etc. None of these spheres is understood without acknowledging a profound relationship between the two components, Iberian and indigenous; and all spheres are centred around the same Christian faith which acquired the power to create culture based on its strong and fundamental roots (even if they are sometimes ambiguous) both ecclesiastic and Catholic.

1.2. Assimilation of the contributions of other cultures

To the first level is added another still more complex in the cultural domaine: there have been successive and, even recently, numerous migrations toward Latin America which not only and generally are diluted into the already existing mixture, but which also are integrated and bring their own contributions, with the help of the religious foundation which they encounter.

Since the sixteenth century, the important African element has appeared, even if through misfortune it came in the form of slavery; however, it is the Church which welcomed and ennobled its strong mulatto contribution, in mixing the African component with the previous population (such as the symbolic figure of a San Martin de Porras) and little by little redeemed its position in trying to save the dignity of the Negro as had already been done with the Indian (here another great symbolic saint appeared, Pedro Claver, as in the previous century the figures of Bartolomé de las Casas, Tata Vasco and so many others had appeared).

Since the end of the 18th century there has appeared, even in territories quite closed off for political reasons, the cultural influence of non-Iberian Europe, first of all French and English, especially under the sign of liberalism; later there was a strong Italian contingent, with another more traditional Catholic symbol; but in all these cases it is the great elasticity of a culture powerfully impregnated with the Catholic Church which has allowed the acceptance - even in curious forms of symbiosis - of new contributions.

Finally, already in the second half of the last century, but especially at the beginning of this one, waves of more distant populations began arriving, such as the Arabs (who were largely Christian and even Catholic) and other Asians (not Christian but who generally assumed Christianity), such as the Chinese, Japanese, and finally - we are pleased to recall it here in Indonesia - inhabitants of the Pacific archipelagos, who moreover had played an important role in those which we today call indigenous; this last fact merits attention because its contributions, not only racial but linguistic and generative of different cultural aspects of production and behaviour, are still today fundamental in the identity of our people and offer extraordinary resemblances which attract the attention of Latin-Americans when we come to these antipodes and when we meet everywhere what we carry in our own blood and hearts.

This successive integration, which is still continuing with new elements from the contemporary era, denotes the dynamic openness which characterizes our cultural Latin-American matrix; openness and dynamism which, as we have said, have something to do with faith, evangelization and the Church, present through numerous forms in the process of cultural encounters.

1.3. Irruption of secularist modernity

During this century, we have seen a recent phenomenon developing in the Latin-American culture, which is usually considered especially as a rupture with the integrating process mentioned above, but which in reality is only a new and dialectical form of the same process. It is the entrance of what has been called modernity, as a cultural fact sealed by the working scientific-technical mentality which has brought the greatest cultural crisis of our history because it concerns our roots and their most intimate and robust values.

These values and roots - as we have categorically stated - are religious and Christian, of Catholic persuasion. Modernity, in contrast, presents itself as secularist and, therefore, does not believe that its basis should be a religious faith; rather it develops an ethos which relegates to the field of sentiment and to the private sphere all that which refers to any possible relationship with the sacred; in culture, then, what is religious is considered as being active only in artistic, folkloric or ancestral expression.

In spite of everything, it is necessary to recall that, although appearing as more secularist, modernity is not a foreign phenomenon to the Christian faith, neither to life in a society protected by ecclesiastical structures; this affirmation is valid not only in relation to the origins of the modern mentality (which have already been studied in theology) but also in all that touches its concrete vigour in our countries, where nevertheless - it must be recognized - it has begun to erode our traditional roots. What has irrupted with this negative characteristic is due in part to the fact that people and institutions of the Church have seen it, unfortunately, above all as an enemy (and all anti-ecclesiastical circles present it as such); but also this is due to the existence of serious cultural lacunae, for whose appearance our Catholic ethos is not entirely exempt from fault, at least by omission.

In fact, there are two aspects to modernity as it appears in Latin America: one is positivistic and pragmatic with stress put on the individual, and comes to us preferably from non-Latin Europe and today especially from the United States; the other is radical, violent and organistic, with an undeniable tendency toward collectivism and even to totalitarianism, coming from Germanic thought and fed today by the Soviet ideology, with certain unorthodox variations. The first aspect clashes with our metaphysical-theological manner of being, rooted in Iberian intellectuality and indigenous spiritual profundity; but it also comes up against our cultural gaps in the face of a practical and productive transformation of nature. The second aspect clashes also with our attitude in religious matters which is personalized, idealized and superhuman; it uncovers, however, the serious gaps in our Christian civilization when faced with the demands for a more just organization of society.

Under this double aspect, modernity presents to us therefore, two legitimate cultural emergencies. We could call them "technification" and liberation. While the first seems to remain removed from the purposes which concern the Church and Christians, it remains, however, a very secular subject, even if it seems less dangerous than at the beginning; as for liberation, it has ended by monopolizing the concerns of the Church, considering that the framework of liberating declarations has increased from the original socio-economic-political sphere toward the educational (liberating education) and toward what is properly religious (theology of liberation), thus reaching the very core of our cultural matrix, although with debatable effects up to now.

2. TASKS OF THE CATHOLIC UNIVERSITY IN THE PRESENT CULTURAL SITUATION

In the second part we will consider the specific tasks suggested to the Catholic university, using as background the entire cultural phenomenon which we have tried to reconstruct up to now.

The report will refer to each of the three stages or levels already described: formation of a mixed cultural matrix; assimilation of the contributions of other cultures; irruption of secularist modernity.

2.1. Saving fundamental cultural roots

I consider this aspect to be a fundamental task, although, as I have said, one simultaneous with others. It is a matter of assuring a stronger and more authentic life force for Latin-American culture; and to do so, concretely, in the face of the extreme and contradictory tendencies of separatist or convoluted "indigenousness" and of the sense of an elitist and alienating Europe.

For our continent, the Catholic university is the institution which has the best opportunities from this point of view: in fact, there is no other Church presence which is more at the forefront, because the university is present on all cultural fronts and not only in its "social advance"; neither is there any other social institution and even less a governmental one, which can be open in this way to the very basis of the most urgent problems of our people.

Consequently, from these facts it is appropriate to point out some practical objectives which stem from this first point:

a) As to <u>subjects</u>: strengthening of the true popular character of our Catholic universities must be a fundamental task, since the "people" are the ones who best retain the double Iberian and indigenous root with all its cultural power.

b) As to <u>knowledge</u> being the purpose of university work: incarnation of the faith must be developed in popular religiosity and in popular wisdom, but also in science for the people, with its two-fold indissoluble characteristic of a civil democratic people and of people with a Church-connected God.

c) Finally, as to the social <u>place</u> of our university
action: we must benefit from this privileged place where
our countries' youth, adult and poor, can construct
a new society on the proper basis and principles, even
if they are not necessarily opposed to those of Europe
or of other parts of the world: a civilization of love
in a continent of hope, according to the instructions
of Paul VI.

2.2. **Maintaining a dynamic openness with regard to other great cultures of the world**

In the present pluralist situation of humanity,
it is very important to promote at the academic level
the immense vitality of our mixed culture, with its
ability not yet adequately exploited to assimilate very
different cultural elements and to dialogue with them.

Here appears the role that rests with our Latin
America to develop in the world dialogue: Does not this
universal dialogue pass today by way of the universities,
more than by way of diplomacy or economics or politics...?
And especially it should pass by way of our Latin-American
Catholic universities where the cultural efforts of
our nations can be sorted out on the basis of knowledge
- research, training, education, "extension to the milieu"
- and in the light of the strongest impulse for knowledge,
the most unbiased, the unique absolute which is religious
faith and, in our case, the Christian faith.

2.3. **Digesting modernity and promoting it from within for an authentic conquest of freedom**

I think here of the freedom of our peoples with
a very strong ingredient of rationality and of "technification" which includes not only the technical-scientific
but also the democracy of coexistence.

Such is the strongest challenge before our young
people. Because without this challenge, the fundamental
roots of our culture cannot be saved (cf. 2.1.) without
losing a little more each time (since the indigenous
person is then seen only as being religious, "primitive",
"superstitious" and the Iberian is seen only as the
"conservative", and the Christian is seen only as dogmatic
and hierarchical): in every case, are seen then only
the paralyzing and backward elements, precisely within
the academic task of the university.

In general a false form of integration of the two aspects of modernity has been given (cf. 1.3.): the positivist aspect is accepted in a great scientific development, but to this has been added as basis an ideology with Marxist tendencies, coming from the second aspect - at a recent period with a certain valorization of the symbolic strength possessed by the religious. But this has created a new dependency, also technological (from the fact of not truly assuming the modern theory-praxis but only its "transfered models") as well as ideological (from the fact of dissolving and weakening the basic cultural values with their transcendent, historical and universal character).

From this point of view, the task of an authentic cultural freedom presents itself thus: freedom which integrates three constellations of values coming from each one of three great constituting stages of our culture:

a) the spiritual, religious, Christian basis of our being mixed, which gives us roots and frees us from inconsistency and vulnerability;

b) the rewarding openness toward other cultures which frees us from a static fixation with ourselves;

c) the assimilation of forces which are scienti-fico-technical as well as economic and socio-political, which free us from the great open gaps within our cultural matrix.

The Catholic Church officially requests universities to work in theory and in practice on this liberating task. As Catholic universities we have the privilege of concerning ourselves with the spiritual Christian base and of giving to it the possibility of dialogue with sciences, technology and various cultural influences, so that faith may continue to show its strength in integrating culture.

For the Catholic universities of Latin America there is opening up the opportunity of relying, for the implementation of this task, on international and transcultural solidarity and collaboration, on the foundation of the same faith, so that, faced with the present difficult challenge, humanity will be more united in its destiny.

+ + + + +

The Role of Catholic Universities in Japan

by Sr. Takako UCHIYAMA
President
University of the Sacred Heart
Tokyo, Japan

A. INTRODUCTION

When the day of Pentecost came round, while they were all gathered together in unity of purpose, all at once a sound came from heaven like that of a strong wind blowing, and filled the whole house where they were sitting. Then appeared to them what seemed to be tongues of fire, which parted and came to each of them; and they were all filled with the Holy Spirit, and began to speak in strange languages, as the Spirit gave utterance to each. (Acts. II 1-4)

Our Faith in Jesus Christ, since the birth of the Church, has found expression in a "plurality" of cultures. The role of Catholic university must, therefore, help this diversity to develop by giving the students opportunities to learn and form a Christian, tolerant and critical judgement on the realities of life as they experience cultural pluralism through their studies in numerous disciplines. Catholic universities, because they are universities and because they are Catholic in nature must assist the Church in safeguarding and promoting this cultural pluralism of the faith, in the light of the Gospel values, and also in being ready to confront the anti-Gospel values in the modern world. In this perspective, I would like now to present my "paper".

B. WHERE ARE WE IN JAPANESE SOCIETY

I. Statistics

First, I would like to invite you to locate the place of our eleven Catholic universities in secular

Japanese society today. Because of the limited time allotted to this report, I have to omit this part. But I have printed out what I wanted to present to you in Documents A, B, C, D, and E.

II. Private Schools in Japan

It is necessary to understand the distinction between the private and public school systems in order to locate the place of Catholic universities in Japanese society. During the long feudal period under the Tokugawa regime (1603-1867), it was private schools (Terakoya) that taught the three Rs to the common people. The private schools had gradually developed until, in 1872, the first system of public education in Japan was established. "The Government Order of Education" organized the three stages, namely elementary, middle and university that we all follow now.

After World War II, more private colleges and universities were accredited. With the characteristics of "independence" and "freedom", the private university today enjoys real academic freedom. It is important to realize that the role of the Catholic university in Japan can only be achieved within the framework of the private universities in Japanese higher education. Since the aim of the private universities is to educate the young to be "good citizens" in the world today so that they will respond flexibly to the demands of society, the purpose of the Catholic universities in Japan can only be understood and accepted as meaningful to present day Japan, when it is grasped in this general movement of the private universities.

C. TO WHAT DEGREE ARE "CATHOLIC UNIVERSITIES" CATHOLIC?

I. The Aim of Catholic Schools in Japan

In today's Japan, when nearly 80% of the intellectuals are graduates of the private universities, the young are more and more "attracted by a school spirit that has been nourished, preserved, and passed down in unbroken succession" such as is found in private universities. This is a big challenge to Catholic universities which have been founded with the clear and definite spirit of their respective founders, to offer the young a Catholic education to prepare them to be realistically contributing members of the global society for a peaceful 21st century. At the same time, we must be aware of

the challenge that we must face, i.e. to what degree
can we universities be Catholic?

In THE CATHOLIC SCHOOL IN JAPAN published in 1985,
Fr. Gustav Voss, S.J., the former head of the board
of trustees of the All Japan Catholic School Federation
said that the role of the Catholic schools in Japan
is to "aim to form the good man". Fr. Voss, when challenged by some for his not having stated that it was
to form the good "Christian", insisted that the overall
policy governing our educational work in Japan must
be "the good man". Of course "the guidance the schools
give is inspired by the Christian concept of man and
is based on the principles and ideas of Christian
thought". However, he continues, "in view of the actual
situation of the Church in Japan, a straightforward
religious education of the whole student body is next
to impossible, because the schools may not expose themselves to the danger of being regarded as mere tools
for just gaining converts. That would create a tremendous
obstacle to the very successful educational and missionary
results which the schools are trying to achieve and,
as a matter of fact, do achieve". In the diversity of
cultural values which make up the secular world of Japan,
the first educational objective is to form a "good human
being".

II. National Incentive Convention for Evangelization

To explore this controversial issue: "To what
degree should Catholic institutions be Christian", we
might look into the draft report of the first meeting
of NICE (National Incentive Convention for Evangelization), convoked by the Japanese Bishops in 1987. It
states clearly that the Catholic school is one of the
most important realms where the light of the Gospel
is introduced into Japanese society. It was an encouraging
phenomenon, that in the course of discussing the mission
of the Church in Japan with a new vision into the 21st
century, the problems of Catholic schools were honestly
faced. There are so many misunderstandings or miscon-
ceptions on the part of the faithful about the Catholic
schools. If Catholic institutions for higher education
want to continue to be accepted and appreciated for
the work they do in a secular world, we must remember
that the academic freedom we enjoy has been earned by
the long and hard history of the private universities
in Japan. To what degree our universities can or should
be "Catholic" in Japan must be correctly gauged in
relation to the cultural pluralism of society, while

facing the social reality of our being a minority group of even less than 0.4% of the whole population of Japan. The direct aim of our institutions therefore is not to make converts, in spite of criticism we receive, such as that there are so few baptisms in Catholic schools, and that the schools do not seem to be helping directly the evangelization effort of the Church.

It is more the basic work of education, i.e. to humanize the people running after material comforts only, that Catholic institutions must aim at in the world-society today. Real Catholic education begins at home. But the case is that most of the parents are not Catholics. Fr. G. Voss speaks strongly on this need that in order "to render the work of the schools really effective, parents should be induced to take an interest and possibly even an active part in the education that their children receive at schools. The children are theirs, not the school's. Parents have the primary right and duty to rear and educate their own children, even after they are enrolled in school. This is a sacred God-given trust the parents must never forsake, a task that neither state nor school, and still less the teachers, can arrogate to themselves". For the university students to come to understand this human duty they have is an important objective of the Catholic universities; in fact, this was the Catholic Education Committee's contribution to the final report of the Ad Hoc Council on Educational Reform convoked by the Japanese Government in 1984 and closed in 1987. This is contrary to the conventional Japanese attitude that school should bear full responsibility and the parents merely cooperate and follow the lead of the school.

D. THE ASPECTS OF THE ROLE OF CATHOLIC UNIVERSITIES IN JAPAN

I. Moral Values in the Family

The basic human role of the Catholic universities in today's world is, therefore, to help the students in building the healthy family of the future, by educating them to be socially responsible and good persons, who can help to bring up the next generation with a solid outlook on life.

The moral vacuum existing in our technologically highly developed society is the main concern for many educators, and even more for those who are Catholics.

Bemoaning the fact of the weak moral training in public schools, many parents desire, more and more, to send their children to private schools, where they believe some solid human values are taught. Many students choose the Catholic universities because they read about the particular spirit of the founders, which appeals to them as offering values in life. Moral rectitude takes precedence over all other considerations very often. One time a student told me that she was happy to have come to our university because she can learn to distinguish what is RIGHT and what is WRONG. Many young today have strong desires for something definite, as they suffer in the uncertainties of social conditions and even in daily human life. Some of them are tired of the changing affluent society and want to be sure of something solid and unchanging beyond the material world.

II. Spiritual Values

The role of Catholic universities in today's Japan, is found here. It is to help them to find real SPIRITUAL VALUES through their studies in different disciplines. Many students confuse supernatural phenomena with spiritual values. The vogue for "occultism" or "fortune-telling" proves that they are drawn to something that they cannot see and to something that is timeless. But this does not mean that they are becoming religious in their outlook on life. Very often those desires for supernatural powers are to help them to obtain what they want in their "egoistic" life. In general people who seek for something above nature have the desire to obtain material favours through super-natural means so that they can enjoy this life on earth. So many new religions (16,246 by 1986) are created but most of them claim to help the faithful to be materially comfortable.

Yet, on the other hand, there is a strong desire to reach peace of mind about the problem of "death". Through the fear of "death", people begin to knock at the door of religion. In a Japanese daily newspaper, recently, there has been a series of articles on "Can Religion Fill/Satisfy the Heart?" The reporter gathers the stories of different people's experiences in life, pursuing their need for and reliance on religion. An episode of a doctor in the Cancer Center of a Hospital tells us that he felt his incapacity to help the patients facing fearful deaths. He left the hospital after his own father's death, to enter the life of a buddhist monk. He is to open a clinic in his buddhist temple to care for old people, physically and spiritually.

He firmly believes that in being a friend to the sick and the needy, the heart of Buddha will pass through from him to them, that they will be liberated from the fear of the sufferings and of death.

Another doctor's story proves that for real medical care he deeply felt the need of both true religion and philosophy. He himself died of cancer, a little later, being baptized a Protestant and in peace with God.

Another young teacher in public school gives an account of her experience in the classroom. She tried to teach the primary school children the value of "life". She had the children write letters to a doctor who could live only three months more. The purpose was to teach them some sense of suffering and death as the meaning in human life, but the teacher had to admit that it was mighty difficult for her to convey such an idea without referring to religion. Since the teaching of religion is forbidden in public school, to these children's questions, like what happens after one's death, etc., she could not fully answer.

While the public schools cannot teach religion, private schools are free to do so. The Ministry of Education strongly encourages the private universities to bring out their respective founding spirit. In order to answer the multi-leveled demands of the young today, the private universities have to live up to their respective distinctive goals set out when they were founded. The time is ripe for us, Catholic universities, to influence the world through our work of education, by helping the students to find real Spiritual Values through religion.

III. Sense of Values

The role of Catholic Universities in Japan is, therefore, obvious in that they should use the freedom and liberty they enjoy in the post-war educational system as Private Universities, by keeping their diversity of characteristics as Private Universities. Catholic Universities can present to the students the true knowledge about "man" and the "world" in the course of different studies. The students can be provided with the opportunities to learn and discover the SENSE OF VALUES. The values cannot be directly handed down to them. The students themselves have to seek for the meanings of the values in multi-cultural life. They must themselves feel the need for permanent values in place of contemporary, relative, changing values which do not give them real meaning in life. How can they learn such values? Only by experiencing, i.e. seeing the values lived. By so doing, the students are being prepared to have the SENSE OF VALUES in life. They must be trained to think freely, independently and fairly without "prejudice" of any kind. It is also the positive contribution of the university to offer its distinctive research and teaching program in each Catholic university. THE DIRECT AIM IS NOT TO MAKE MORE CONVERTS. The work of the university is to present truths in various disciplines, so as to make the students able to form a solid philosophy of life themselves, based on a coherent sense of values. We continue operating Catholic universities, because we believe that women and men will all be given a chance of choosing God, Truth and Light and Goodness, at their last moment in life. It is my firm belief that for this final choice in life, we prepare our young people.

An important value we must implant in the students is the sense of "human life". It is the duty of the Catholic university to influence the youth today in Japan to have respect for life. Japan is known as being a "heaven for abortion". It is a sad picture. We should fight against this fearful and blasphemous state of affairs, as a social and world and global evil. We must give the students the intellectual as well as ethical knowledge, to reject as human beings such brutal behaviour. If the adults of the next century have no respect for human life and dignity, there will be no future for Japan. Every means should be used to inculcate this truth into the minds and hearts of the Japanese youth now. The task is urgent in the global world of today.

IV. Gospel Values

The role of the Catholic university is to present GOSPEL VALUES against materialism, so that the opportunity is amply offered to them to have a choice of values in their life-time. The more comfortable and rich the world becomes, the more people suffer from the meaninglessness of life. Our task, and also our challenge, is to lead the students to come to the knowledge that there is a definite and positive meaning in life in "the symbol of Cross", a Christian symbol. The vertical line of the Cross is the relationship between God and man. The horizontal line shows the world of human relationships which are often the cause for problems in life. The relational horizontal line and the vertical line are to meet in life on earth. This is the meaning of human life. This meeting between the two lines must be experienced in every day life by every human being. Catholic education must provide the students with the realization that this meeting, this crossing of the two lines of relationships is the Key for personal integration in one's life.

V. Sense of Internationality

The role of Catholic University is also to implant the real SENSE of "INTERNATIONALITY" in the soul of the young. It is not enough to teach them many foreign languages, nor to present them with knowledge about other worlds in this Universe, but to consolidate in their heart the truth of human life, that all men are equal. Before God, there are no Jews, no Romans... The spirit of openness to everybody on earth can lead them to be freed from the "prejudices" which are the main evil preventing the world becoming ONE PEACEFUL WORLD. It is a tall order, but if the Catholic university fails in making an effort to enable the young to overcome their "prejudices", it were better not to establish any such distinctive university whose main philosophy of education is Christian. This true spirit of "internationality" is, therefore, a positive contribution that the Catholic universities in Japan can bring into the world of higher learning today.

E. SENSE OF SOLIDARITY FOR PEACE IN THE WORLD

Lastly, I would like to conclude this paper with the message of the Holy Father addressed to the present day youth on the Day of Peace in 1986, because in this message, the objective goal of our Catholic universities seems to be well and tersely summarized.

I invite you to join with me in reflecting on peace and in celebrating peace... as the universal desire of all peoples everywhere... we are one human family. By simply being born into this world, we are of one inheritance and one stock with every other human being. This oneness expresses itself in all the richness and diversity of the human family: in different races, cultures, languages and histories. And we are called to recognize the basic solidarity of the human family as the fundamental condition of our life together on this earth... To recognize the social solidarity of the human family brings with it the responsibility to build on what makes us one. This means promoting effectively and without exception the equal dignity of all as human beings endowed with certain fundamental and inalienable human rights. This touches all aspects of our individual life, as well as our life in the family, in the community in which we live, and in the world. Once we truly grasp that we are <u>brothers and sisters in a common humanity</u>, then we can shape our attitudes towards life in the light of the solidarity which makes us one. This is especially true in all that relates to the basic universal project:

PEACE.

Peace is always a gift of God, yet it depends on us too. And the keys to peace are within our grasp. It is up to us to use them to unlock all the doors!

+ + + + +

Number of Catholics

	Catholics	Population	Percentage of Catholics
1920	76, 404	55, 963, 053	0. 136%
1925	84, 804	59, 736, 822	0. 142
1930	92. 798	64, 450. 005	0. 1436
1935	105, 165	69. 254, 148	0. 155
1940	119. 224	73. 114. 308	0. 163
1945/46	108. 324	71. 998, 104	0. 154
1950	142. 461	84. 114. 574	0. 169
1955	212. 318	90, 076, 594	0. 235
1960	277. 502	94, 301, 623	0. 294
1965	323, 880	99, 209, 137	0. 326
1970	356, 252	104, 665, 171	0. 340
1975	377. 687	111, 939, 643	0. 336
1980	406, 796	117, 060, 396	Q. 345
1985	432. 805	121. 048, 923	0. 357

Catholics: Catholic Bishops' Conference of Japan (1986. 12. 31.)
data of 1946 instead of 1945 (no data 1941-1945)
Population: "'85 Population Census of Japan"
by Statistics Bureau, Management and Coordination Agency

Document B

Universities and Junior Colleges

1986	National and Local-Public			Private		Grand
		(National)	(Local-Public)		(Cath.)	Total
Univ.	131	(95)	(36)	334	(11)	465
	29. 2%			71. 8%	(2. 3%)	100%
Jr. Col.	89	(37)	(52)	459	(31)	548
	16. 2%			83. 8%	(5. 7%)	100%

from "Monbu Tokei Yoran 1987"
by Ministry of Education, Science and Culture

Age Pyramid for Japan (1980)

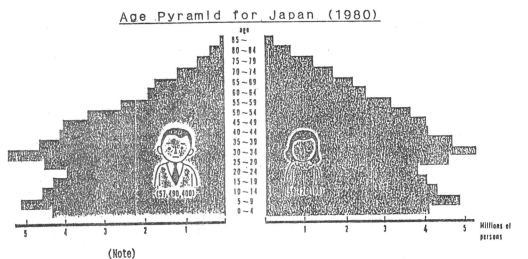

(Note)
Population 116,916,400
Density of Population per 1 km^2 314.4
Number of Households 34,083,200
Members per household 3,3

from "Education In Japan"
by Ministry of Education, Science and Culture

Enrollment of Catholic Schools

			1982	1983	1984	1985	1986	1987
UNIVERSITIES	NUMBERS		12	12	12	12	12	12
	STUDENTS	Male Total	10,561	10,459	9,907	9,652	9,815	9,564
		Male Catholics	342	317	309	312	335	314
		Female Total	15,542	15,691	15,679	16,060	16,818	17,128
		Female Catholics	855	803	830	778	815	757
	PROFESSORS	Priests	179	180	172	172	188	183
		Brothers	3	3	3	4	2	2
		Sisters	98	90	98	110	102	92
		Laymen Catholics	280	250	264	359	340	329
		Laymen Non-Catholics	1,347	1,118	1,200	1,668	1,629	1,595
JUNIOR COLLEGES	NUMBERS		33	33	33	31	31	30
	STUDENTS	Male Total	1,335	1,380	1,423	1,295	1,285	1,287
		Male Catholics	43	46	52	50	24	39
		Female Total	13,103	13,394	13,396	12,557	13,236	14,049
		Female Catholics	438	472	469	361	395	347
	PROFESSORS	Priests	46	50	42	36	27	36
		Sisters	2	2	3	5	0	4
		Brothers	175	164	168	168	161	161
		Laymen Catholics	207	192	217	211	171	178
		Laymen Non-Catholics	628	715	725	755	752	691

Catholic Bishops' Conference of Japan   (1987. 12. 31.)

Document D

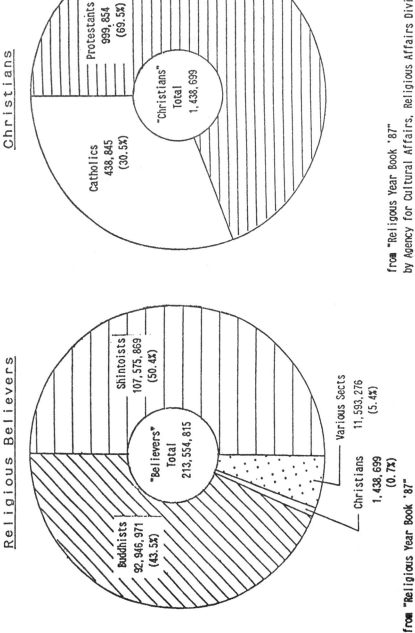

Christians

Protestants
999,854
(69.5%)

Catholics
438,845
(30.5%)

"Christians"
Total
1,438,699

Religious Believers

Shintoists
107,575,869
(50.4%)

Buddhists
92,946,971
(43.5%)

"Believers"
Total
213,554,815

Various Sects
11,593,276
(5.4%)

Christians
1,438,699
(0.7%)

from "Religious Year Book '87"
by Agency for Cultural Affairs, Religious Affairs Division (ed.)
Catholics: Catholic Bishops' Conference of Japan (1986.12.31.)

from "Religious Year Book '87"
by Agency for Cultural Affairs, Religious Affairs Division (ed.)

New Religions in Japan

Year	Romanized name	Japanese
1838	Tenri kyo	天理教
1919	Ennou kyo	円応教
1926	Kikueikai kyodan	菊栄界教団
1930	Seichou no Ie	生長の家
1929	Nihon keishin suso jishudan	日本敬神崇祖自修団
1935	Sekai kyusei kyo	世界救世教
1948	Chushinkai	へ心会
	Shinseikai	真生会
1922	Houraisan seishin kyo	蓬莱山誠神教
1931	Ekido kyo	易道教
1944	Perfect Liberty kyodan	パーフェクトリバティー教団
1946	Tensha tsuchimikado shinto honcho	天社土御門神道本庁
1946	Zenrinkai	善隣会
1947	Tensho koutai Jingu kyo	天照皇大神宮教
1945	Nihon Ehoba kyodan	日本エホバ教団
1946	Shinrei kyo	神霊教
1947	Hachidai ryuou daishizen aishin kyodan	八大竜王大自然愛心教団
1930	Tensokou kyo	天祖光教
1944	Makoto no Michi	真の道
1948	Shinsenreido kyo	神仙霊道教
1949	Seiko kyo	聖孝教
1949	Izumo shintou yagumo kyo shinjiinkai kyodan	出雲神道八雲教神心会教団
1944	Tenchi no taikyo	天地之大教
1941	Seikyokai	聖教会
1946	Uchu motohajime shinkyo	宇宙元始神教
1946	Sekai heiwa kyodan	世界平和教団
1923	Fumyokai kyodan	普明会教団
1949	Kyuseishu kyo	救世主教
1956	Daishizen tenchi hi no ookami kyo	大自然天地日之大神教
1949		

timeline axis years: 1830 1840 1850 1920 1930 1940 1950 1960 1970 1980

from "Religious Year Book '87"
by Agency for Cultural Affairs, Religious Affairs Division (ed.)

Original: Brasilian

THE CHALLENGES PUT TO THE CHRISTIAN FAITH

BY MODERN-CONTEMPORARY CULTURE

by Marcello AZEVEDO, S.J.
Rio de Janeiro, Brazil

The central theme of this XVIth General Assembly of the International Federation of Catholic Universities (IFCU) is "Faith and Culture: the Role of the Catholic University". The subject I have been asked to develop belongs therefore in the context of the total programme and refers specifically to the first part of the general theme. It should, nevertheless, serve to provoke and make possible the treatment and discussion of the second part which is linked to the identity and the objective of the group assembled here.

The university was born in the integrating context of the great medieval syntheses, although it already contained the seed of the subsequent gestation of that which we call modern culture; the latter would affect and transform it profoundly in the course of history, especially in recent times. The Catholic university - as we understand it today - emerged in the modern university context. But as a Catholic university it comes within the ecclesial framework, indeed inspired by and rooted in a non-modern cultural context. Not only, then, in that which concerns its own identity and goals, but also its functional character, is it important for the Catholic university to be aware of the challenges presented to the Christian faith by modern--contemporary culture.

I intend to delimit first of all the semantic field of the three elements which make up the theme of this talk: Christian faith, culture, modern-contemporary. I shall go on then to identify some fundamental traits of the internal structure of modern-contemporary culture. The selection of these data is linked to the specific nature of the Assembly and consequently to the primary significance of these features for the Catholic university. Finally I shall point out some of the challenges presented in our time to the Christian faith by this modern-contemporary culture, at the level of the relationships between faith and knowledge, faith and the person, faith and praxis. The choice of these three levels of challenge has taken into account the further development of the Assembly with respect to the role of the Catholic university in the context of the relationship between faith and culture.

I. SEMANTICS

A. CHRISTIAN FAITH

This term is not confined here

- to the intellectual content of the faith;
- to doctrinal expression of the faith;
- to theological research on the faith;
- to liturgical and spiritual expression of the faith;
- to ethnico-moral dimensions of the faith;
- to the religious complex of institutionalization of the faith.

Here Christian faith is understood as the existential response of welcome and acceptance given by a human person to the living reality of Jesus Christ. In him and through him God and the human being manifest themselves to each person and to human-kind as a whole. This response encompasses the total life of a person. Every human person is located within a social and cultural context. Jesus himself came at a specific time in history and in a defined geographical space, within the socio-cultural framework of a particular people. As a result the Christian faith is a personal and relational human experience which finds its expression and significance at the social and cultural level of human life. As such it is historical and immersed in history by its very nature.

Given, therefore, its personal, human and historical character, the Christian faith,

* inasmuch as it is related to the concrete reality of Jesus, should be open to the human experience as it is lived in all and each of the various cultures; otherwise its universal significance and the fundamental human meaning of Jesus Christ and his Gospel would fade away;

* inasmuch as it is related to the concrete reality of human persons, should have a significance and socio-cultural expression within the different socio-cultural contexts which exist in the world;

* inasmuch as it is related to human persons in a socio-cultural context, has a cultural dimension and its expression is a definite praxis which derives from the experience of God and of the human person, an experience lived in and through Jesus Christ.

There is, then, an intimate and necessary relationship between faith and culture, between individual faith and the socio-cultural experience/expression of this faith.

B. CULTURE

This term is not understood here as

- an effect of human action on nature;
- a creative manifestation of the human spirit translated into art, poetry, sculpture, architecture, music: humanistic sense;
- research and accumulation of knowledge: education;
- a phenomenological manifestation of the way of life and the behaviour of a human group (language, crafts, cooking, dress, dance, songs...): folkloric sense;
- an ethnological expression of the human diversity within the various social groups (the group

itself being thus a "culture"): ethnological sense.

Culture is understood here as the **set of meanings, values, models, symbols and patterns, incorporated into or underlying the action and communication of the life of a specific human group.** This ensemble is lived by the group, consciously or unconsciously, and assumed by it as a characteristic expression of its own human reality. It passes from generation to generation as it was received, or transformed - actually or supposedly - by the group.

It is at this deep level of cultural roots (the level underlying the expression of the phenomenon) that the relationship between faith and culture is found. For this reason, the process of evangelization ought to be at the same time a process of inculturation. An "inculturated" evangelization which seeks to arouse and develop the Christian faith should therefore reach the very heart of culture. It must do it starting from the mutual relationship and interaction between the faith and the basic presuppositions of culture. Consequently, evengelization as a relationship between faith and culture cannot be limited to the intellectual reformulation of the contents of the faith nor to the mere adaptation and accommodation of the expressions of the faith (rituals, liturgy, signs, discipline and method).

The rupture between faith and culture at this deep level of interaction constitutes the drama of our time, as indeed it did of former times (Evangelii nuntiandi). This breach leads to an internal dichotomy between faith and life, both in the individual person and in the cultural and social context in which believers act and communicate with each other. Dissociated from life, faith remains void of its ethical consequences. It will not lead therefore to a coherent Christian praxis. This decisively influences the formation of the individual conscience and the configuration of social and political structures.

Through a process of inculturated evangelization which is respectful and critical, dialogic and dialectical, the gospel message may succeed in becoming a new source of inspiration stemming from the very core of the presuppositions of culture. Thus a culture emerges which is at the same time new in its perspective and faithful to both its original and deep human cultural teleology and the liberating and transforming action of the Spirit.

C. MODERN-CONTEMPORARY

This term is not meant here as

- modernity, in a philosophical sense;
- modernity, in the ideological sense referred
  to by the Marxist critique of liberal and capi-
  talistic ideology, as opposed to the socialist
  and communist ideology;
- modernity, in the technological sense of substi-
  tution of techniques and processes;
- modernization, in the liberal-capitalistic perspective of the "theory of modernization" imbued
  with the ideology of progress/development/growth;
  its fundamental presupposition is the linear
  evolutionary process which leads to the transition
  from "traditional" to "modern" society.
- modernism, neither in its literary and artistic
  sense nor in its theologico-historical sense.

Modern-contemporary qualifies here the comprehensive
culture - that is to say the cultural reality as understood above: the sum of meanings, etc. - which may be
identified as such under its empirical, historical,
analytical and structural aspects, and distinguished
from the comprehensive non-modern culture. Modern and
non-modern in culture can coexist in the same society,
but their cultural paradigms or universes are clearly
distinct and identifiable as such.

It is possible to trace back the remotest roots
of the constitutive process of modern culture, in which
complex historical factors of multicultural integration
are involved. This process began in the XIth century
in the culturally diversified geographical space that
today corresponds to Western Europe. Western Christianity
was at once the catalyst of the process and the determining protagonist of its evolution. Although structurally
non-modern in this phase, this process of cultural
mutation was characterized by significant breakthroughs
which prepared the ground for the emergence of modern
culture. Some of these profound cultural changes were
later incorporated in the internal structure of the
said culture.

The constitutive process of modern culture was
accelerated throughout the XVIth and XVIIth centuries
and was consolidated specifically in the XVIIIth and

XIXth. This historical and cultural progression involves numerous protagonists and a range of diverse elements. For, in effect, during the Middle Ages modern culture developed slowly and in embryonic fashion, defining itself more and more until eventually, with the various revolutions - scientific, industrial, electronic and the computer revolution -, it established itself. The stages were numerous: the Renaissance, the Enlightenment, and the contrasting liberal and revolutionary movements and tendencies; the American, French and Soviet revolutions; the philosophical watershed of Descartes vis-à-vis Scholasticism, and its later development under the name of modern philosophy, whereby it encompassed extremely diversified and even contradictory trends of thought; natural and social science; the economic ideologies and processes which began with the monetary and commercial revolutions of the late Middle Ages and eventually materialized since the second half of the XVIIIth century and throughout our time with their theoretical development ranging from Mandeville to Marx, from Adam Smith to Milton Friedman; the autonomy of the secular States, the creation of the nation-States, and later the implantation of the socio-economico-political systems, whether capitalist or socialist, in their many versions, models and nuances, and in their various historical materializations especially in the XIXth and XXth centuries; colonial expansion and neo-colonial pressure whether economic or political or both; the expressions of this complex historico-cultural process in the arts, literature, the system of education and research, and in the various forms of understanding, formulating and expressing religion; and, over and above, the slow and <u>protracted</u> movement which was the profound transformation of the daily life of the people, at the same time generator and receiver of the processes of socio-cultural mutation, of the subtle exchanges or violent clashes of meanings and values, of symbols and intuitions, of norms and patterns, of techniques and methods, of new ways of acting, communicating and behaving.

By the very nature of the cultural process, this historical progression did not conform to static or permanent paradigms. On the contrary, the process was and still is open to new changes. Crises and conflicts are inherent in the identity of modern culture. In spite of these contrasting trends and factors, however, and thanks to the intense process of such constant and profound transformations, modern culture is firmly rooted in some fundamental presuppositions which form its internal structure. These presuppositions find expression in different ways in the daily life of the people, both in modern societies and in those which undergo their impact and influence.

These cultural elements or fundamental presuppositions allow us to identify modern culture as well as its correlation and comparison with non-modern culture. Moreover these elements continue to be basically present in the new cultural category globally termed post-modern. The critical reading and posture vis-à-vis the modern define in greater part the post-modern without for all that modifying radically their common fundamental presuppositions. So it can be said that the modern paradigm involves clear cultural breaks with respect to the non-modern, when both are considered globally and specifically. In relationship to the post-modern paradigm though there is a basic continuity of the modern that remains, although its fundamental elements are corrected and reoriented, reformulated and restated, as a result of the critical perception of the modern by the post-modern.

The use we make here of the term modern-contemporary renders it possible to embrace, without further qualification, this dynamic complexity of continuous change within modern culture as it has been developing in the course of its past and in the midst of the crises of the present, pressing on towards that which will continue to be its own transformation in the future. Change is inherent in the modern cultural process and results from the dynamic of some of its own presuppositions.

Moreover, in designating this culture as modern-contemporary we perceive and emphasize more clearly the distinction between on the one hand modernity as culture (modern culture) - which is my cultural-anthropological approach here - and on the other hand modernity in its various acceptations already indicated: philosophical, ideological, humanistic, ethnological and technological.

II. THE INTERNAL STRUCTURE OF MODERN-CONTEMPORARY CULTURE

Without claiming to be exhaustive I shall now mention some basic elements or presuppositions of the internal structure of modern-contemporary culture.

1. The centrality of the individual, considered as subject of rights, decisions and actions. The indi-

vidual has his/her intelligibility and legitimation without a necessary reference to the group or any dependence on it. Accordingly, an accent is placed on the equality of individuals and on individual liberty as well as on the formation of the individual conscience and on personal responsibility. The contrast between individual attitudes and interests may lead to competition, to a lack of solidarity, in the context of the "ideology of individualism". It may also, in virtue of the relational nature of the person, make possible an openness towards the community with active signs of individual autonomy.

2. Secularization, which is a central feature of modern-contemporary culture, can be seen

- either as autonomy of the immanent which rejects a comprehensive legitimation and intelligibility to the universe, through the mythic or religious element, and leads to a cognitive and axiological independence which is very far-reaching and has vast concrete repercussions;

- or as the fragmentation of the comparatively homogeneous and organic universe of meanings and values, of symbols and patterns, which characterizes the comprehensive nature of non-modern culture.

3. This fragmentation leads to a plurality of universes each of which develops its own relatively autonomous epistemology, methodology, vocabulary and discourse, which are not linked up with analogous constellations within an integrated whole. The result is pluralism which in modern culture is not primarily a manifestation or effect of tolerance, but rather a structural consequence of this autonomy of different universes in the process of interaction. Modern pluralism requires discernment and dialogue and can benefit from a dialectical approach aiming at a possible overcoming of conflicts and contradictions. Sometimes it may also lead to polarization and radicalization.

4. Ideology can be seen here as the absolutization of a partial perspective which attempts to present itself as universal explanation and legitimation. This understanding of ideology underlines the interest of certain groups that seek to impose or legitimate their actions and goals. Ideology can also mean the cognitive and axiological basis as required by the various universes for them to become intelligible or to establish them-

selves. This is a fundamental requisite for the intelligibility of both a vision of the world and a partial perspective of knowledge or interpretation. In either sense _ideology_ is an essential feature of modern culture. Its one-sided exacerbation could lead to the modern phenomenon of totalitarianism in its different degrees and versions.

5. The mutual feedback between _science and technology_ as a structural datum of modern-contemporary culture contributes to the constant _changes_ which characterize it. Today's technologies, especially the most advanced ones, are in general systematic and affect the individual and collective consciousness, with an impact on daily life. In this way they excercise a notable influence on culture and society in their entirety. To deal with this impact it is important to analyse, firstly, the internal structure and scope of the scientifico-technological processes in themselves and in their forms of gestation and implantation; this allows an adequate reading and interpretation of the final phenomena or products, together with their ethico-moral evaluation.

6. The significance of _mathematics_ as a common language and lingua franca among the different sciences has a profound effect on people's minds especially through its abstract, symbolico-formal nature and expression. The decisive importance of mathematics in our time may have a double side effect: first, the reluctance to understand different symbolic languages even to the point of rejecting or underestimating people who use them; second, a tendency to avoid the ethical consequences of human decisions which were made on a purely mathematical level without further consideration of their economic, political and social consequences.

7. A dynamic conception of an ongoing _history_ as opposed to the vision of a static or cyclical history which characterizes non-modern culture. In the latter the human being is subject to history and in a certain manner suffers it, being defenceless before it and quite incapable of transforming it or giving it a new direction. In the modern conception the Christian consciousness of relationship to time, a relationship seen in historical and eschatological terms, can find itself clashing with a notion of time merely intramundane and exclusively immanent. On the contrary, the integration of the historical and eschatological dimensions helps to linking faith and life in the real universe of modern culture.

The aforementioned structural features, without being exhaustive are significant for the question we are dealing with: to detect the challenges presented to the Christian faith by modern-contemporary culture in the perspective of a Catholic university.

Furthermore, I would like to underline two important points:

* Firstly - We find ourselves today in the middle of an obvious crisis of modernity, in many different forms some of which relate to the critique of one or other of the elements mentioned above. Yet I believe that, even though the crisis is undeniable, it is still very much localized in small groups which perceive it and attempt to cope with it. The crisis of modernity is far from being translated into terms of macro- and microscale to the point of considerably affecting the socio-cultural fabric of current world's daily life.

* Secondly - Although I have said it before, I repeat here my claim that many aspects of that which is today called the post-modern, as a possible new cultural paradigm, neither deny nor invalidate the internal structure of modern-contemporary culture as we have presented it. The so-called post-modern trends adopt a critical posture towards the elements of this structure and endeavour to correct their aberrations or perversions, or indeed reorient them teleologically. They retain, however, some of their valid intuitions such as the value of the individual and the person with its consequences, at least at the theoretical level, of equality and freedom.

III. THE CHALLENGES PRESENTED TO THE CHRISTIAN FAITH BY MODERN-CONTEMPORARY CULTURE

From the preceding description of the structural elements of modern-contemporary culture we can conclude that this culture is at once a solidly integrated phenomenon and a fragmented reality. In effect, there is on the one hand a consistent interdependence and interaction between the principal dimensions of this culture: its secularity, its mathematical approach and the mutual feedback between science and technology.

There is as well a planetary expansion of these dimensions since they have been diffused by international trade, by economic, political and military interdependence, by the scientific method and the standardization of research, by the educational process, and by the systems of information and communication. All this makes of modernity a strongly integrated cultural phenomenon. On the other hand, we are aware of other modern structural basic assumptions such as the autonomy of the individual, pluralism and ideology with their consequences. From this point of view modern culture appears to us as an actually or potentially fragmented reality.

The nature of modern-contemporary culture is then complex, all-pervasive and diverse, whether its trends and currents may be or may have been at different periods and in various situations. Therein lies, indeed, its fundamental challenge to the Christian faith in our times. It is this cultural whole, at once well-constructed and coherent, fragmented and changing, localized and wide-ranging, that constitutes, as a whole, the great challenge thrown down to the basic question: Can Christianity, the Christian faith and message, have a meaning for today's world? Can they survive in it? Can they find in this cultural setting any conditions not just of residence side by side, either tolerated or confronted, but rather conditions of mutually critical and dialectically integrated growth?

Never had Christianity to ask itself in such a radical way questions as these, never in the face of any other culture whatever among the many it has encountered and in which it has been inculturated or acculturated throughout its history. Springing up itself in a non-modern cultural context, it moved around culturally among equals, especially during the first millennium. Early in the second millennium, it gave rise to a Christian culture, of Western European extraction. Such a culture which was the result of a multicultural synthesis came to be diffused throughout the world and sometimes imposed upon various peoples by the correlated process of colonization and evangelization. It was in this culture with a Christian background that modern culture took root, which would in its turn evolve through a divergent process in global contrast with the Christian matrix of its inspirations.

The lack of perception of this original and extensive nature of modern culture - at least in Latin America and possibly in other parts of the world - leads to reductive approaches to this culture by both the institutional Church and Catholic universities. This also allows the harbouring of expectations, without any basis in the long run, of an eventual return to a non-modern cultural paradigm. This would be expressed, for example, by a return of the sacred, by an ecclesial and theological uniformity, by an authoritative Church position on secular issues, by the cultural post-modern claim of a full break with the basic assumptions of the modern culture.

The Catholic university currently seems to be one of the qualified actors to reach a complete and accurate knowledge of modern-contemporary culture and to help the Church to take heed of it. This entails certain precise demands for interdisciplinarity procedures and intercultural dialogue between teacher and student subcultures within the university itself. It also requires a critical posture by the university with regard to its own submissive attitude towards modern culture. Such submission might not be intended and could be attributed to the ideal of simply being a university for our time. It demands, finally, that the critical process begin in the very heart of modern assumptions and not only or always start from a counter-cultural attitude or an alleged return to the non-modern culture. Here, then, we have the first and major challenge put to the Christian faith by modern currents, a challenge that a Catholic university must be concerned with.

There is a second challenge, one that is crucial in Latin America and perhaps also elsewhere. It is the isolation of individual goals, the dynamic of personal self-fulfilments entirely dissociated from the context and social consequences of a generalized poverty and oppression, of structural violence and injustice in that continent and in the world. This thrust comes from the "ideology of individualism", a perverted development of the value put upon the individual person by modern culture. This tendency is clearly noticeable in the attraction and markedly functional aims of certain careers such as business administration, computer science and various branches of engineering, main sources of immediate return and reliable promise of status and self-assertion in the short term.

The epistemological, methodological and operative orientation and guidelines of these disciplines and careers tend to strengthen the secularist perspective of modern culture. They make viable the individual's social mobility, but as a rule they do not take heed of or go deeply into the social significance and responsibility of the individual's promotion, thus aggravating the injustice and stratification of society instead of contributing to overcome them.

Quite a number of universities, whether Catholic or not, struggle with this forceful intrusion of the market as a determinant factor, if not an exclusive one, at the level of the academic selection of students and the pedagogical orientation of teachers. The only way out of such an impasse would come through an intense communication between the university and the actual society, and not merely between university and the research/teaching operation, on the one hand, or between university and the applied science/enterprise on the other hand. Furthermore, it is important to foster an active cross-fertilization between the natural/exact sciences and the human/social sciences. That interaction will gradually lead those different universes to a realistic sensitivity to the urgency of social change. Otherwise we shall be confronted more and more by a double dichotomy: on the one hand, natural, exact and technological sciences; on the other hand, human science, social science and aesthetics, all of it in the mute, conformist, sterile impermeability of epistemologies, methodologies, languages and interests (first dichotomy); on the one hand, the scientific and academic universe; on the other hand, the universe of the faith, as an immobilized and conservative one, as a meaningless and ineffective realm (second dichotomy). The individual perspective, therefore, and its projection onto the university are a second big challenge presented to the faith by modern-contemporary currents.

This second challenge is completed and made specific by a third. The dissociation between faith and life dissipates and relativizes the demands of an ethical projection of the faith. This rupture has been a distinctive feature of Latin America down through its history and for the greatest part is at the roots of its present dramatic situation. The rupture between faith and life explains the existential contradictions of persons, institutions and societies which publicly profess the Christian faith while quietly living hand in glove with injustice, violence, poverty and oppression, or even fostering them.

In a world which is structurally pluralist there is an established right to make oneself heard in terms of one's very identity. Therefore, the Catholic university should not perpetuate that rupture between faith and life. On the contrary, the university should face up to that reality and boldly make understandable to the contemporary mind and heart the integrating linking of faith and life in theory and in practice.

In Latin America this process of integration is made difficult by two assumptions which are mutually exclusive. On the one hand, there is an ideological identification of modern culture with the secularist, liberal-capitalist tradition. This leads to a limited and inadequate notion of modern culture and to an acritical underestimation of its real significance in the present world. On the other hand, there is a drive for urgent changes, rooted in an equally secularist and materialist perspective, or not, which more or less emphasizes the immanent and therefore inworldly objectives, often excluding implicitly all transcendence. These two trends make impossible a true Christian praxis that may be effectively liberating and transforming. Both remain closed to an ethical projection of the Christian faith.

The specific worldview of a Catholic university should find concrete mediations leading to a praxis, that is to say, to a conscious construction of history which is clearly inspired by the Christian faith and flows from it. This entails the already mentioned overcoming of a privatized faith, one that is exclusively oriented towards the intimate experience and expression of the individual person. It also helps people to go beyond a reductive or ideological analysis or interpretation of modernity. Indeed, modernity should be considered as a pervasive cultural reality that sometimes coexist with several non-modern cultural paradigms. These two cultural patterns however are clearly distinct from each other. Moreover we should bear in mind that the structural, basic assumptions of modern culture equally underlie the two major, ideological traditions which split the world today and contend for it: the liberal-capitalistic tradition and the Marxist-communistic tradition. Finally, the worldview of a Catholic university should bring about a conscious appreciation of the political dimension of the Christian faith. Only thus can one arrive at this integrated relationship between faith and life which allows us to project it into the process of reconstruction and reformulation of both the socio-cultural fabric and the economico-political mediations.

With the recognition of the differences, but also the annulment of the irreductible dichotomies between private and public, between the spiritual-subjective and the actual socio-political-objective, the ethico-Christian linkage will be possible. In that way, therefore, the correcting and surmounting of elitism, stratification, discrimination and marginalization in societies and institutions will be effected, and indeed in the university itself. Likewise the conditions necessary for the building of a just and sharing society at once profoundly human and for this reason basically Christian will exist. The Catholic university, as a university and as a Catholic one, plays a key role both in the inspiration of this project and in its implementation.

+ + + + + + +

Original: English

THE CHURCH AND THE ECONOMIC CRISIS -

SOCIAL DOCTRINE OF THE POPE CHALLENGES WESTERN CULTURE

by Gregory BAUM
Montreal, Canada

At this time we are witnesses of a curious paradox in the life of the Catholic Church. In matters relating to the inner workings of the Church the message of the Vatican is extremely conservative, while in matters relating to the social and economic order Vatican teaching is bold and radical. When Pope John II speaks of ecclesiastical issues he adopts a conservative attitude that distrusts decentralization and participation, and yet when he speaks of secular issues he becomes a radical democrat insisting that people are meant to be the responsible subjects of their societies.

In North America in particular, John Paul II has a conservative image. People know about his traditional views on women and sexual ethics, his emphasis on authority and obedience, his displeasure with public dissent, and his preference for a highly centralized Church. Yet what people do not realize is the radical nature of his economic and social theories.

The conservative stance taken by the Vatican at this time, at odds with the spirit of the last Council, has begun to worry a significant sector of the Catholic Church. A lecture given to the representatives of Catholic

colleges and universities might well examine the difficulties the Vatican's conservative stance creates for
Catholic academic institutions. If the Vatican had its
way, our universities would become glorified ecclesiastical seminaries. Fortunately recent events seem to
suggest that if Catholics get organized and resist on
the basis of sound Catholic principles, they are able
to make the Vatican modify its policies.

While this conflict deserves careful attention,
it is not the subject I wish to examine in this presentation. I want to deal instead with the paradoxical
counterpart, the Church's critical social teaching.
The present address is an appeal to Catholic colleges
and universities to take seriously and make available
to their students John Paul II's radical critique of
modern society. The dominant values on North American
university campuses, including Catholic colleges and
universities, tend to be "neo-conservative" ones,
legitimating the existing economic and political order.
Catholic educators do not always recognize this very
clearly. In the present world crisis I attach enormous
importance to the Church's social teaching.

* * *

Allow me then to begin by offering a summary of
John Paul II's social analysis of the present economic
crisis. This analysis has been endorsed and developed
by the Canadian bishops and, less consistently perhaps,
by the American bishops as well. According to the encyclical, Laborem exercens (1981), world capitalism is
entering upon a new and brutal phase which unless stopped,
will dispossess and disenfranchise widening sectors
of the world population.

Prior to World War II, at different speeds in
different countries, capitalism was becoming a more
benign economic system. The Great Depression had convinced
people that capitalism was an essentially unstable system,
subject to economic cycles, and that for this reason
governments should extend a helping hand to the industries
during periods of decline. Capitalists were eventually
willing to enter into an unwritten contract with society:
in return for government assistance, they promised to
support full employment, welfare legislation and respect
for labour organizations. This more benign phase of
capitalism was enormously successful for a time. It
produced great wealth in the industrialized countries.

It created the hope of upward mobility among ordinary people. People felt that if they themwelves did not make it, at least their children would.

This phase has come to an end. The unwritten contract with society is coming apart. Unemployment is steadily rising, welfare legislation is slowly being dismantled, and labour organizations find themselves attacked from all sides. The gap between the rich and the poor, and more especially between rich countries and poor countries, is ever widening. What is taking place, according to the analysis of the Pope and the Canadian bishops, is a giant effort on the part of the capitalist class to rebuild the economy on an international basis around the privately-owned, giant corporations. These corporations are no longer committed to the well-being of the society in which they were originally based. On the contrary, they have become so powerful that they can exert pressure on governments and influence national policy.

The Canadian bishops describe this process in some detail. They point to the changes taking place in the structure of Canadian capital. They show that capitalism following its own logic, now no longer restrained by a commitment to the common good, creates centres of power that enrich themselves at the expense of the less developed hinterland. This process empoverishes the developing countries of the South: and in the North, the same process creates unemployment and regional disparity and thus widens the gap between the rich and the poor.

In their pastoral letters the Canadian bishops describe this system, but they avoid the term "economic imperialism". In Canada this word has a decidedly Marxist ring. Yet John Paul II does not have this scruple. He roundly condemns the "imperialist" orientation of liberal, i.e. unrestrained capitalism. On his trip to Canada he castigated economic and political imperialism in a provocative manner.

In his most recent encyclical, Sollicitudo rei socialis, John Paul II repeatedly points to the "mechanisms" built into the economic structures that produce the increasing maldistribution of wealth. They are called "mechanisms" because they are at work quite independently of people's intentions. They operate according to a logic of their own. The Pope calls them "structures of sin", a concept taken from contemporary liberation theology.

The ills of the industrialized North, in capitalist and in communist countries, - so John Paul II says - are due to the violation of a basic ethical principle: the priority of labour over capital. The priority of labour over capital is observed when the industries are made to serve those who work in them and beyond them serve the labouring society as a whole. In capitalism and in communism this priority is not observed. In capitalism the decisions regarding the use of capital are made by owners, managers, or board of directors in view of enhancing private wealth and power, and in communism the economic decisions are made by government bureaucracies in view of enhancing the political power of the totalitarian state.

To assure the priority of labour over capital in the developed North, John Paul II does not advocate revolution. He believes instead that both capitalism and communism can be significantly restructured. While he severely condemns liberal or unrestrained capitalism, he thinks that the Western economic system can be substantially modified by allowing it to become more democratic, i.e. by increasing the participation of workers in ownership and decision-making. He entertains the same reformist hope for communist society. The socialist system can also be transformed through greater democracy. John Paul II calls for an economy organized on a non-ideological basis, i.e. a mixed economy with some public ownership, some private ownership, some worker ownership, and some community-based ownership. Ultimately he envisages the industries to be worker-owned.

And who is the historical agent to introduce these changes in the societies of West and East? According to John Paul II it is the labour movement, the organized workers conscious of their historical vocation. And it is the moral duty of all who love justice, to support labour in this struggle. John Paul II calls for the solidarity of labour joined by the solidarity with labour.

In Sollicitudo rei socialis, the Pope deals specifically with the inequality between the developed North and the developing South. Why is the South sinking into ever greater poverty and powerlessness? John Paul gives two answers. The first cause is the organization of world capitalism to enhance the wealth of the industrial and financial centres in the North. This is the point already mentioned above. The second cause is the division of the North into two blocs, related to two empires, both of which promote an ideology that claims to be universal. Both ideologies are defined as absolutes, both therefore are idolatrous. The clash between these competing ideologies, liberal capitalism and collectivist communism, produces a dynamics of hostility that leads to the **"cold war"**, to smaller wars by proxy, and to preparation for nuclear war.

The division of the North into two hostile blocs, each pursuing an absolute, has a devastating impact on the South. Countries in the South that want to free themselves from the colonial net and start their own development have to decide between one or other side of the two blocs. And in doing so, they tragically enter into the destructive East-West dynamics. The two empires in the North understand the South not in terms of its own problems, but in geopolitical terms, in terms of their own East-West conflict. Since the countries of the South have to choose between the two blocs, their populations become easily divided over this choice: these countries are thus weakened by internal conflicts, conflicts that sometimes even lead to civil war. John Paul II rages against the ideological bi-partition of the North as one of the principal causes of the world's ills.

The Pope even argues that the dominant ideology in the two blocs blinds the ruling classes in regard to the fact that the system they extoll no longer serves their own societies. Again this is true in East and West. In regard to Western societies John Paul II underlines the unhappy social conditions, conditions described in detail by the American bishops in their pastoral on economic justice and the Canadian bishops in several of their pastoral letters. Capitalism embraced as ideology creates unemployment, housing shortage, poverty, and social deterioration, and at the same time blinds the successful sector of society in regard to these effects. The ideologues keep on praising their system without looking at what is actually going on in their own society.

Against this trend, John Paul II preaches a new ethic of solidarity. We must rediscover that we belong to one another, that we are one another's keeper, that we are responsible for one another, that we are engaged in a joint historical project to build a just society. What the Pope calls for, especially in <u>Laborem exercens</u>, is a **"preferential"** solidarity, a solidarity extended to workers and the dependent sector of society first, to produce a social movement that will restructure society according to greater justice and eventually create the historical conditions for a solidarity that is truly universal.

* * *

The Church's official social teaching goes against the cultural mainstream of the Western nations. In North America this teaching finds the support of the Canadian and the American bishops' conferences. But it is received only by a minority of Catholics. As a matter of fact, the ecclesiastical critique of society and the new ethics of solidarity were first worked out by groups of Christians at the base. These Christians are grateful that their radical social gospel has been accepted by the Church's magisterium.

But when the new ethic of solidarity is preached in parishes and introduced in Catholic schools, the majority of Catholics tend to be embarrassed. They see their society from the perspective of the dominant culture. They are ill at ease with the Pope's ethical critique of capitalism. The same embarrassement is found in Catholic colleges and universities. Usually only small groups of students and professors receive the Church's teaching and apply it to the various academic disciplines. These groups sometimes form small organizations to promote social concern on the university campus, often without the support of the president and the administration. I know Catholic colleges where president and faculty while claiming to be very "Catholic" actually oppose the Church's social teaching. In many instances, I suppose, economic needs force the university to become indifferent to the burning social issues of the age.

The new orientation of capitalism analysed in the ecclesiastical texts is accompanied by a neo-conservative culture that blesses and legitimates it. In North America and Great Britain in particular, we are continually told that society has been too generous in the past, we have given too much away, that we helped people instead of allowing them to become self-reliant and inventive. Today we have to recommit ourselves to free enterprise. We have to relearn that we must look after ourselves, that we are responsible for our own careers, and that society should allow the ambitious and enterprising to succeed. It is they, the entrepreneurs, who are the wealth creators in society. They deserve our respect and admiration. Governments should get off their back. Instead of impeding their creativity through taxes, governments should promote private corporations by granting them tax concessions and removing the social and legal obstacles that stand in their way, in particular the privileges of labour. What is needed is a flexible labour force. Workers have to learn again that life is tough. This is no time for free lunches. If we want to compete on the world market, we will have to tighten our belt. People will have to learn to do with less. In the present situation, high unemployment is normal and natural. In the future workers won't be able to be so fussy. New welfare laws will oblige them to take work, any kind of work, even if it does not lead to a steady job. And so forth. This is the message we hear.

The neo-conservative culture tries to reconcile us with inequality. It teaches us to shrug our shoulders with a good conscience. We rely on intellectuals in the social and political sciences to devise theories explaining that the way things are, are the way they have to be, that history takes place according to fixed laws and that human agency is largely an illusion, or that contentment can be found only in accepting one's limitations and searching for spiritual consolation and that the utopian dream of a just society betrays an irresponsible absence of realism. And then we have scientific theories that tell us that the poor nations have only themselves to blame for their poverty and that the marginal and defeated in Western societies have failed because they did not try hard enough.

Against this cultural sweep stands the call of the Catholic Church for a new ethics of solidarity. The Catholic Church is supported in this by Geneva-based World Council of Churches. It is joined by other religious and secular movements. What I am suggesting in this paper is that Catholic colleges and universities should assimilate the preferential option for the poor and investigate what its meaning is in the various academic disciplines. The preferential option offers a new hermeneutic that has a profound effect on the whole intellectual enterprise. In my opinion, the shift in the Church's official social teaching is an important historical event, possibly of global significance.

+ + + + +

Original: English

THE TASK OF THE CATHOLIC UNIVERSITY

IN THE DIALOGUE BETWEEN FAITH AND CULTURE

by Arij A. ROEST CROLLIUS, S.J.
Rome, Italy.

As the title of this paper indicates, its scope is practical. When we speak about a task, we speak about praxis. Theory is presupposed. This presupposition is justified in this particular gathering, and also after the prestigious conferences that have been presented here.

Even if the scope of this paper is modest, treating it requires boldness. The attempt to present operational conclusions and practical propositions in the context of the variety of cultures where Catholic universities exist can involve over-simplification or over-reaching in the treatment of the topic. Both these extremes have to be avoided. A way to avoid extremes is to remain close to reality. For this reason, a first articulation of this paper presents the reality of the Catholic university as a meeting-point of faith and culture. In a second part, the dynamics of the dialogue between faith and culture will be discussed, stressing what one could call **"the anthropological mediation"**. The concluding section presents some practical consequences for the life and activities of a Catholic university.

85

1. THE CATHOLIC UNIVERSITY AS MEETING-POINT BETWEEN FAITH AND CULTURE.

This title evidently contains a misleading simplification. On the level of universities one cannot speak of "culture" in the singular. Universities, because of the nature and variety of their disciplines and because of the composition of faculty and student body, write "**culture**" only in the plural.

A second remark to be made is that the dialogue between faith and cultures is much wider than what happens at a university. A Catholic university is a meeting-point and not the meeting-point in this dialogue. It is a very specific meeting-point. This specificity has to be brought out here.

The specific role of the Catholic university in the dialogue between faith and cultures is given with its very nature and identity. The words "**catholic**" and "**university**" both mean an all-encompassing openness, but each of a different nature. And it is the union of these two kinds of radical openness which constitutes the specificity of the Catholic university. "**Catholicity**" implies the radical openness for the totality of Life and Truth God has shared with humankind in the dialogue of salvation which culminates in the person of Jesus Christ. And "**university**" signifies the radical openness for the totality of technical, artistic, intellectual and sapiential disciplines by which humankind has been formed and has given shape to its world and society. In both cases, the radicality of the openness does not regard only the past. Neither does it merely express that, given the immensity of both fields - that of the dialogue of salvation and that of human cultures - the openness is only radical, and therefore always to be perfected. But the openness of both "**catholicity**" and "**university**" is also said to be radical because of the horizon toward which it is expanded in each case. The culmination of the dialogue of salvation in Jesus Christ does not mean the conclusion of this dialogue, but rather a new beginning, with a new covenant to which all human beings are invited. And the totality of human cultures is not first of all to be sought in the monuments of the past but rather in the convergent projects and concerted efforts by which humanity grows toward its true identity and makes the world more human. "**Catholicity**", therefore, and "**university**" are basically future-oriented.

In both cases, moreover, the specific openness denotes another difference. In the case of **"catholicity"**, the radical openness is one faith. This means, concretely, fidelity to the word of God as it lives in the Church and to the Church that is called together by this word. As to **"university"**, the radical openness is one of study, research and reflection. Concretely, these activities are undertaken in view of education. Education, be it technical, artistic, intellectual or sapiential, can be said to be the primary cultural activity, and culture the final fruit of education.

The meeting and **"constellation"** of the openness of faith and that of culture is a privileged instance where human beings assume the fullness of their responsibility in being God's cooperators in perfecting the creation toward its becoming a **"new creation"** and in forming women and men toward their becoming a **"new humanity"**. Because of the radicality of its openness and the encompassing width of its horizon, the Catholic university can be considered as the primary and privileged place of the dialogue between faith and cultures.

In this brief sketch of the reality of the Catholic university two remarks still have to be made. The first bears on the plurality of cultures. This plurality does not only involve the variety of cultural traditions that can meet within one university, but means also, and even in the first place, the differences resulting from the processes of cultural change by which generations can be distinguished. The process of education exists precisely by virtue of these cultural differences which are bound to exist between faculty members and students. Tensions, and even gaps, are healthy stimulants in cultural growth.

A second and final remark corresponds to the beginning of this first section, where it has been stated that **"culture"** has always to be written in the plural in the context of the theme studied here. The question could arise: and what about faith? Should this not also be written in the plural, precisely because of the radical openness that has been mentioned? The answer to this is that, because of the radicality and totality of the openness of faith, it can only be written in the singular. There is only one dialogue of salvation. But the faith in which the divine initiative in this dialogue is received and answered is not the exclusive privilege of the members of the Catholic Church. This is because the divine initiative in this dialogue has been expressed and perceived **"in many and various ways"**. Also the belonging to the Church is not restricted to baptised Roman Catholics, but is realised in various ways and degrees in other Christians and in followers of other creeds.

The Catholic university, therefore, precisely because of its catholicity, welcomes and needs the collaboration of non-Catholics in the dialogue between faith and cultures.

2. THE DYNAMICS OF THE DIALOGUE BETWEEN FAITH AND CULTURES.

2.1. The Anthropological Mediation.

This section is an attempt to answer the question **"How do faith and cultures enter into dialogue?"** For our present purpose, there is no need to repeat the basic principles that have been written here and there about the process of inculturation. The thrust of the papers and discussions in this gathering suggest that one fundamental reality should not be lost sight of, and that is: human reality. As Fr. Azevedo has pointed out, the relationship between faith and culture centres upon the human person and, since culture is a social reality, this relationship involves the human person-in-society.

As the specific topic of this paper is the task of the Catholic university, we have to keep in mind what universities are about: research, teaching and, one might add, experimenting and living-out. Research, teaching and experimenting involve reflection upon reality. Human reality is reflected in the **"image"** one conceives of the human being in its socio-historical setting. It is this **"image of man"** that constitutes the mediation between faith and cultures in the dialogue that is the endeavour of the Catholic university. In this image we have the anthropological mediation in the dialogue between faith and cultures. The dynamics of this dialogue is centred on this mediation.

The dynamics of dialogue implies a movement in two directions, formally opposed, and, because of the existent mediation, complementary. In university teaching and research, this means, on the one hand, the **"transposition"** or **"translation"** of the image of man resulting from Christian experience and from the Christian documents of faith into the language of human cultures, and on the other, the **"assumption"** or **"integration"** of all authentic human values found in the various cultures into this same image of man. The criterion for discerning these values on their authenticity is operative in the very dialogue where faith and cultures meet, and involves the arduous task of research, also in the way of experimenting and living-out, in the light of the faith as it is lived and handed-on in the Church.

2.2. The Christian Image of Man.

Within the framework of a Catholic university is basic here the task of biblical and theological anthropology in the reflection on the Christian image of man. The Second Vatican Council, in its Pastoral Constitution on the Church in the Modern World Gaudium et Spes, has presented the essential traits of this image. In one word this can be resumed: man is the image of God. The image of man is, first of all, the reflection of the image of God as revealed in Christ. In the words of Gaudium et Spes: **"Christ, the final Adam, by the revelation of the mystery of the Father and His love, fully reveals man to man himself"** (n.22). Thus, in the development of the Christian image of man, christology has a **"critical function"**, especially with regard to all that is ambiguous in the image of man and humanity as it evolves throughout history.

In the elaboration of the image of man, four types of categories have an important role. They should be mentioned briefly here.

2.2.1. The Categories of Origin and Perspective.

The human being is, at the same time, a given reality and a project. As a given reality it points to origin and historical experience. As a project it implies calling and destiny. These categories have their full sense in the history of salvation. Thus are to be affirmed the divine origin and the transcendental destiny of humanity and each human person.

2.2.2. The Categories of Conflict.

These categories flow forth from the preceding ones, and help to describe the historical experience of humankind. Promise and project have been endangered by human infidelity and disobedience. The concrete image of man, therefore, has to be depicted with the oppositional categories of slavery and freedom, of ignorance and revelation, of sickness and healing, of death and life.

2.2.3. The Categories of Commitment.

Truth can only be acknowledged by a personal act and sets free the human person as such. Truth and veracity in knowing self and others is what constitutes the authenticity of the human person. Truth is also the faithfulness of love. The main personal categories are those of justice, service and sacrifice. The Christian image of man is signed by the Cross of Jesus Christ.

2.2.4. The Categories of Hope.

Christian hope is founded upon the divine promise and upon love that is stronger than death. In this context the categories of happiness and fulfillment, of peace and of communion are important.

With the terms belonging to these four categories, or the denial of them, all creeds are formulated, all history is written, all poems, dreams and dramas are conceived, ideas and ideologies are expressed. If Origins, Conflict, Commitment and Hope are the four main points of reference of the image of man, based upon the authentic **"revelation of man unto himself"** in Christ Jesus, then the dialogue between faith and cultures has to take into account this structure of the anthropological mediation. The **"translation"** of this image in the various cultures while assuming their values and the **"assumption"** of the values of human cultures into their own experience and reflection, which constitute the dynamics of this dialogue, will, therefore, be structured according to these categories. It will now be possible to draw some practical conclusions with regard to the dialogue between faith and cultures in Catholic universities and to present some operational propositions.

3. THE ROLE AND TASK OF THE CATHOLIC UNIVERSITY IN THE MEETING BETWEEN FAITH AND CULTURES.

3.1. The Main Thrusts of the Dialogue Between Faith and Cultures.

The role and function of the university are of an essentially dialogal nature. Doing the work of a university means exercising a civilising function at the meeting-point between generations and between cultures. This civilising function is realised through teaching as the fruit of research, experimenting and reflection, and bears directly on the technical, artistic, intellectual and sapiential disciplines formulated in the various cultures of humankind.

The specificity of the Catholic university consists in the image of man that constitutes the inspiration and ideal in the exercise of this civilising function. Given the basic future-oriented character of the university, it follows that the Catholic university can be seen as a workshop ("atelier") of a new and authentic humanism. This humanism is formulated, in each generation and each culture anew, in the process of **"translating"** and **"assuming"** that is characteristic for the dialogue between faith and cultures. Hence it can be said that the dialogue between faith and cultures constitutes the very identity of the Catholic university. The task of the Catholic university that is discussed in this paper is then nothing else than the task of being -and therefore ever more becoming - what one is.

The four types of categories that have been distinguished above are also the points of reference for indicating the <u>main thrusts in the dialogue between faith and cultures</u>. In the first place, the transcendental categories of origin and perspective stimulate those who collaborate in a Catholic university to be open for all cultures without fully identifying with any given one insofar as it is precisely a **"given one"** and not also a project that opens up to a transhistoric fulfillment. With such a perspective, ideal can never harden into ideology, and cultural identity never be exchanged for the caricature of cultural apartheid. Both ideal and identity can only exist in a dialogue of which are excluded only those who refuse dialogue.

The categories of conflict are closely connected with the refusal of dialogue. A Catholic university is a place of research and discernment which, in the ultimate instance, is a spiritual discernment. All those factors and elements in cultures that bear the mark of slavery, ignorance and death have to be acknowledged and confronted. Such confrontation sometimes can be a healthy storm in a situation of constructive dialogue, but can also lead to the very denial of dialogue. Such a denial can never be final, and it is precisely one of the tasks of creative university research to find ways to overcome obstacles in this inter-cultural dialogue. Let it be noted that such obstacles are not only found in the dialogue with representatives of other religions or ideologies, but can also exist within the context of Catholic universities themselves.

Given the categories of commitment, the Catholic university will work at and transmit a humanism in which the human person has a central position without this humanism becoming a form of individualism, and which contributes to building human society without it becoming a mere collectivism.

In line with the categories of hope, the Catholic university will form agents of communion and workers for peace: women and men who find their fulfillment in the service to their fellow human beings.

Thus one sees that the **"radical openness"** which is characteristic for the Catholic university, as has been mentioned above, takes on a concrete shape in these main thrusts of dialogue. And with this also the main obstacles in this dialogue become manifest. In the first place, there is the obstacle of isolation, be it in the form of religious exclusivism, cultural apartheid or exaggerated specialisation. This isolation can be self-imposed by a narrow dogmatism in one of these areas, but it can also be the result of ideological impositions coming from outside the university. In this last case, the dialogue will be characterised by an unrelenting struggle for the vindication of academic freedom. This academic freedom is not an end in itself, but is the indispensable condition for the elaboration of an image of man that, while corresponding to the unalienable insights and promises of the Christian faith, can be translated into the language and value systems of other cultures while assuming all their authentic values. This elaboration is not the work of one single seminar or course, but is an on-going process, which has also its moments of uncertainty and obscurity. Academic freedom, therefore, goes together with academic patience, whereas dogmatic or utilitaristic attitudes are often characterised by impatience. The impatience to see immediate results is another impediment in this endeavour of dialogue. Furthermore, in the context of the dynamic tension between person and society, there exists, within the concrete set-up of a university, with its many and heavy programmes, the possibility of a lack of creativity.

Creativity rarely is found in commissions and boards, but it is rather a matter of personal endeavour and of spontaneous association of persons. University structures do not always facilitate personal initiatives. Without creativity, the dialogue between faith and cultures can be an interesting academic exercise, but will do little for the designing of an image of man in which cultures can meet and toward which they can work and walk together. This image of a new humanism, though known in its basic traits, is still largely to be discovered, invented, created. On the side of the surrounding society, an obstacle in promoting a genuine dialogue between faith and cultures can be a form of cultural conformism, different according to the different cultural contexts in which the Catholic university is found. The process of discernment between values and non-values within the contextual cultures is a task that is necessary for the survival of the Catholic university as such. A final obstacle in the elaboration and promotion of a new humanism as task of the Catholic university can consist in a spirit of merely individual self-promotion among those who frequent the university. When service to fellow human being does not become one of the great ideals of our students and their genuine vocation, the university has done very little in the way of dialogue between faith and cultures.

3.2. Operational Propositions for the Promotion of the Dialogue between Faith and Cultures as the Task of a Catholic University.

These final remarks do not intend to indicate some themes for eventual seminars or workshops, neither to run ahead on the conclusions of this Assembly. Their intention is to highlight some of the practical implications of the central function of the anthropological mediation in the dialogue between faith and cultures.

3.2.1. Inter-university collaboration.

A first element that presents itself, inspired also by the very fact of this meeting, is the need to strengthen the collaboration between the universities that are united in the International Federation of Catholic Universities. In view of the various symptoms of cultural provincialism, the mere fact of the existence of our Federation is a message. But in order that this message have a greater impact, we need practical proposals in order to widen the channels of various types of communication and of exchange and meeting of people in research and teaching.

In this context, the importance of the Centre for the Coordination of Research might be underlined. In the measure that this Centre creates and develops networks of correspondents around the world that creatively assist in identifying the important issues that require our attention, it fulfills a function that is vital for the existence of our Federation.

3.2.2. Collaboration with Universities of Different Inspirations.

In elaborating the image of man that corresponds to authentic human values, the academic collaboration of scholars and research persons belonging to different creeds or ideologies is of the greatest importance. It would be essential for any given Catholic university to have in this a universalistic approach, and not to limit the collaboration to just one type of interlocutors. This more universal openness can also be a safeguard against exaggerations in cultural conformism and against simplifications by losing sight of the complicate structure of the spiritual landscape of our world.

This collaboration already is taking form, in several of our universities, in exchange of students and professors, in the framework of agreements of academic cooperation. Moreover, precisely in view of a common or - at least - convergent view of human existence and destiny, there is an immense and urgent need of promoting common research projects. Such research projects often bear on the one of the four types of categories used to express the Christian image of man. Besides the elements already mentioned, it may be useful to recall one or two of the recommendations of the Symposium organised by the Centre for Coordination of Research in September 1985 in Tantur/Jerusalem on "Inculturation: The Christian Experience amidst Changing Cultures". It was then proposed to convoke another symposium, on the transforming potential of religions in situations of social injustice. It had also been recommended to support research programmes on the participation and the role of women according to various cultures.

3.2.3. University Courses in "Christianity".

In many universities there exist courses in Islamology, Hindology, Buddhology, etc., for students who themselves do not belong to these religions. (The fact of the existence of these disciplines and this type of intellectual curiosity in one given culture and the absence thereof in most other cultures would be worth investigating.) Nowadays, there are more and more non-Christian students and scholars who want to study Christian religion and culture, as an academic discipline. They are not really helped by theology courses that are offered to Christian students. In the present dialogue between faith and cultures, the Catholic universities would render a great service, which they alone can render, if there could be, in every major cultural area, a university with a program in Christian religion and culture, specially for non-Christian students.

3.2.4. A Theology of Pluralism.

One of the recommendations of the Jerusalem Symposium in 1985 has been to encourage theologians to clarify in their research and in their teaching how pluralism (in theology, liturgy, Church structures and spirituality) belongs to the very catholicity of the Church and is the articulation of its unity. It would be very important to involve in such research also theologians from the Oriental Churches, which have a longer and more intense experience of pluriformity. Such a study would be vital for a fruitful dialogue between faith and cultures in our present situations.

3.2.5. The Ethics of Service.

Since the attitude of putting oneself and one's talents at the service of others, without discriminating among them, is and should be a characteristic of the formation programmes of Catholic universities, we would help each other if, in a practical way, we could formulate what is meant by an "Ethics of Service". If we say that we are training leaders, and we don't train them for service, then we are only talking. Motivational workshops on "service" at our universities would contribute in a significant way to an effective dialogue between faith and cultures.

3.2.6. International Research Project on Solidarity.

The recent Encyclical of Pope John Paul II, Sollicitudo rei socialis, undoubtedly constitutes a challenge for an international academic meeting as ours, which has as its main objective to put in evidence the relevance of the Christian faith with regard to the cultures of humankind. This Encyclical contains various pages of "culture criticism", especially where it deals with the "sinful structures" of modern society. Moreover, the implications of solidarity as an answer to some of the greatest socio-economic problems of today have also to be worked out. It would seem that our meeting cannot remain deaf to the intellectual challenges of this Encyclical. Hardly any other gathering can be thought of which is so well equipped to conceive, follow through and bring to a fruitful conclusion a global and inter-disciplinary project of research on the main questions raised in the papal document.

3.2.7. Spirituality and Technology.

Another of the Jerusalem recommendations which seems too precious to be forgotten in the files, where the reports of meetings are gathering dust, proposed an interdisciplinary workshop on Christian spirituality in the tension between traditional forms of spirituality and the life of persons in an electronic age. Such a workshop could also be an opportunity of collaboration with scholars from non-Christian religions.

3.2.8. Cultural Change and Ongoing Formation.

Fr. Azevedo's paper mentioned the increasingly rapid pace of cultural change which is characteristic for the modern times. Ongoing formation is no luxury in such a situation. Our universities have here a unique opportunity to be at the service of modern women and men. High-powered study sessions for Church leaders, business executives, technocrats and politicians are already organised here and there and would have to be multiplied. Experience should be pooled. Self-renovating programmes have to be invented. This would be a very efficient and practical way to contribute to the dialogue between faith and cultures.

3.2.9. Formation of Communicators.

Because of the "anthropological mediation", the dialogue between faith and cultures is a form of social communication. The human person is essentially a commu-nicator. Many of the symptoms of cultural isolation, dogmatic rigidity, lack of academic freedom, unreflected conformism, etc., which have been mentioned above, are in one way or another connected with a deficiency in communication and in the ability to communicate in an effective way. The sciences and arts of communication, on the technical, artistic, intellectual and sapiential levels, form a priority in any formation programme at the service of the dialogue between faith and cultures. In this case especially, cultures have to be written in the plural, and intercultural research would be of immense value. In no other respect is the human person to such a degree culturally influenced and differentiated from others as in his being a communicator.

A research programme for which many of our universities are particularly well situated and equipped would concern the religious and sapiential traditions in the various cultures as "systems of communication". Also ideologies would have to be considered in such a project. These systems operate by the means of rites, story-telling, instruction, etc. A programme like this would be interdisciplinary, with the collaboration of cultural anthropologists, specialists in communication studies, theologians, politologists, etc.

The list of operational propositions could be lenghtened. Those that have been mentioned here are more directly related to the theme of the present meeting. Several of them do not need the setting up of new structures in order to be realised. But we could draw on the existing resources and programmes in our universities. The only thing required would be to do some intelligent "networking", and to find one practical person to keep such a network alive and productive.

One final remark can serve to further clarify the scope of these propositions. The international collaboration between our universities is not only a uniquely effective instrument for promoting the dialogue between faith and cultures. Our real collaboration is also the affirmation of a central reality in this dialogue. This reality is the universal validity of the new humanism, inspired by our faith and to be worked out in our manifold activities on university level. Our very being together here confirms the universal validity of this humanism, which englobes an immense variety of cultural expressions, mutually enriching in their convergence, and in their divergencies stimulating dialogue.

+ + + + +

Original: English

THE TASK OF THE CATHOLIC UNIVERSITY

IN THE DIALOGUE BETWEEN FAITH AND CULTURE

IN A PLURAL MULTIRELIGIOUS SOCIETY

(The Indonesian Experience)

by Frans SEDA
Jakarta, Indonesia

My observations are based on the Indonesian situation and experiences. I have no pretentions to speak on behalf of Asia or other developing countries, although Indonesia has all the characteristics of a plural, pluralistic and multireligious society common in Asia: pluralism in races, language, cultures and religions.

From the viewpoint of relationship between Faith and Culture, the history of the development of the Indonesian society shows the following stratification.

The oldest layer is the indigenous stratum generated by a mixture of migrants from South China/Indochina with the indigenous negroid tribes of this archipelago, some 15.000 years ago. There is harmony between Faith and Culture; it is the so-called **"cosmic totality"**.

This indigenous Faith and Culture has spread throughout the archipelago and has still influence in the inland regions all over the country.

The second stratum of Faith and Culture is the one influenced by the Buddhist and Hindu religions from India, since the beginning of Christian area, and now still influencing life and culture in Java. It is dominant in Bali.

The third stratum of Faith and Culture is the one influenced by Islam which came to this country in the 12th century and which is dominant in Sumatra, Java, coastal areas of Kalimantan, South Celebes and North Maluccas.

The fourth stratum of Faith and Culture is the one influenced by Christianity which came to this country in the 16th century. Christianity mixed in with the local indigenous cultures; most of them had not yet been influenced by Hinduism or Islam in the eastern part of Indonesia. Nowadays there are 170 million people spread over around 17.000 islands, with hundreds of languages, a diversity of cultures and traditions and 5 officially recognized religions (Islam, Protestantism, Catholicism, Hindu, Buddhism).

Colonialism came and introduced the so-called Colonial Culture, with its drive for westernization, modernization and secularization. But colonialism has also promoted, although not purposely, nationalism, national independence and the search for National Identity and National Culture.

80 years ago, the "**Boedi Oetomo**" (Prevalence of Mind) was founded. The Indonesians look on it as the starting point of shaping modern Indonesia, culturally, socially and politically.

This modern Indonesian culture is the pursuit of the principle of Unity in diversity (not unity and diversity). The challenge is how to promote unity while preserving diversity, and how to preserve diversity in support to unity. This fundamental challenge is altogether the fundamental framework and reference for the dialogue between Faith and Culture in this country.

It is obvious that Indonesian Catholic Universities are influenced by the diversity of cultures, religions and traditions where they are located. In the process of modernization, the location in a rural or urban environment makes also differences between the various universities. Students, teachers, professors, university staffs of all walks of life are cooperating together.

In the 10 Catholic Universities with their approx. 35.000 students, 19.250 students (55%) are Catholic and 15.750 students (45%) are non-Catholic. From 848 full-time teaching staff, 80% is Catholic; from 3.700 part-time teaching staff, only 25% is Catholic. That is why the University Campuses are ideal places for the meeting of minds, the dialogue and cooperation between persons and generations of the nation with different religious, faith, cultural and traditional backgrounds, in a formal and informal way: ideal places for educating and cultivating the sense of unity in diversity, and sense of cooperation and joint responsibility for the common good.

Because of the special and unique position of Faith and Culture in Indonesia, the Indonesian Catholics have developed an attitude of openness towards society, towards other religions and faith. Catholic institutions are institutions initiated by Catholics and inspired by or in the light of the Gospel but open for and to serve Society and the Nation as a whole. We are a minority without the Ghetto mentality. As it is told to our Catholic leaders by Father van Lith, S.J., the **"guru"** of Indonesian Catholics, in matters of national culture and nationalism in the 20's, Indonesian Catholics should be 100% Catholic and 100% Indonesian.

This is the way we are pursuing the permanent and dynamic dialogue between Faith and Culture.

The problem is how to preserve and to develop this attitude in a changing society. Then one has to know what is the thinking behind it. For this, one has to go back to fundamentals, to fundamental views, insights and requirements, basic in the relationship between Faith and Culture.

From the Indonesian condition and experiences one can derive two basic themes in the dynamic and permanent dialogue between Faith and Culture in a plural and multireligious society:

1. The dialogue between the (Christian) Faith and Culture. The process of inculturation.

2. The dialogue between the Christian Faith and other
   Faiths behind the Culture(s). The interreligious
   dialogue.

The terms faith, religions, Church, Christianity
are here used not in a systematic way. However one should
be clear about their specific characteristics. Faith
is the acceptance and readiness to give a personal
response to a relationship with God, or a Being/Power
above the human being.

Religion is faith incorporated into daily life,
regulating relationship to God, to the neighbour and
to society, with a set of rules, worships, rites and
rituals, with rewards and punishments. Not all religions
have a clearcut faith.

- Church is structured and institutionalized religion
  with leadership (with or without Hierarchy) and
  membership, guardian of the patrimonium of faith (only
  in Christianity).

- Christianity/Christendom (Islam, Buddhism, Hinduism),
  an organic unity, a movement, an ideology based on
  religious values striving for human well-being, by
  influencing society, life, culture and aspirations.

I. THE DIALOGUE BETWEEN FAITH AND CULTURE:

I.1. Dialogue between (the Christian) Faith and Culture
     in a plural, multireligious society. The process
     of Inculturation.

     1.1. Faith is God-given. Culture is man-made. How
          the twain shall meet.
          Faith should be developed into culture. Other-
          wise it is not fully discerned, fully thought
          and fully lived. Culture is needed to preserve
          faith. On the other hand culture is developed
          around a faith. Culture can only survive by
          the faith it possesses. Faith is the soul
          of culture. Culture without faith is culture
          without spirit, without life.

     1.2. But a dialogue, especially a permanent and
          dynamic dialogue needs more than this simple
          knowledge about the fundamental relationship
          between Faith and Culture. The dialogue is

a process in which positions and attitudes during the **"meeting of the twain"** (between faith and culture) are decisive.

1.3. In the history of Christianity, the five following attitudes between Christianity and Culture are recognized.

    1.3.1. An antagonistic attitude, based on a collision course between Christianity and culture.

    1.3.2. An attitude of dominating. The Christian faith should dominate culture.

    1.3.3. An attitude of accommodation. The adjustment of Christian faith to cultural conditions.

    1.3.4. An attitude of dualism. Faith and culture are two separate things. No relationship between them.

    1.3.5. An attitude of openness to culture, to transform culture for the human well-being. In Catholic language, the so-called Inculturation.

Although these attitudes are developed in the Western Christianity, they are relevant to the attitudes in the Church of developing countries because historically Christianity came to those countries from the West. It is accepted that Inculturation is the official attitude implied in the teachings of and should be implemented after Vatican II. But in promoting Inculturation we can still observe an antagonistic, or a dominating, or an accommodative, or a dualistic approach, which makes the problem and the process of Inculturation more problematic and more complicated.

The task of the Catholic University is to assist scientifically the purification of the approaches and to come to an authentic process of Inculturation, which is a two way traffic rather than a one way traffic between Faith and Culture. A process of penetration and integration. The task of scientific purification is also needed to select what and which aspect of the culture should be integrated. There should not be more culture and less faith, or the other way around, more faith and less culture.

These tasks of the University should be done in the framework of an open, permanent and dynamic dialogue.

The task of the University is also to promote, to maintain and to develop this open, permanent and dynamic framework.

I.2. The dialogue between the (Christian) Faith and (other) Faiths beyond the culture(s) of a plural and multireligious society. The interreligious dialogue.

This is apparently a "**conditio sine qua non**" for a fruitful and productive dialogue between the Christian Faith and Culture in a multireligious society.

2.1. Theology has a dominant role in this kind of dialogue. As in the case of theology there are three traditional approaches in the Church in the dialogue between religions in a multireligious society.

2.1.1. The antagonistic approach. Only the Church has the truth, the other religions are "**heretical**". The richness of their values are irrelevant to the truth of the Church. Critics of this approach point to its negative orthodoxy.

2.1.2. The approach from the viewpoint of the uniqueness of Christianity. While recognizing and taking other religions seriously, the Church does not need to open its doors to them because of the uniqueness and perfectness of revelation of the Christian religion. Critics of this approach show that it is based on a narrow historical dimension and neglects the dimension of GRACE in other religions.

2.1.3. The open approach to other religions with full recognition of their heritages and their usefulness in support to the Christian value, theological, philosophical system. This is based on the belief of the dimension of grace in other religions, and on the recognition that they can be used by God as "**media saluti**" (although not perfect and not complete) in the building of His Kingdom.

We have to clarify for ourselves our basic approach and attitude in order to be respected by other religions as a trustful partner in the dialogue.

Catholic Universities have the task to discern, to clarify and to promote the open approach towards other religions and the theology behind the open approach without falling into syncreticism.

2.2. Besides the theological handicap to interreligious dialogue, there is the historical, psychological barrier, caused by Colonialism with its culture of westernization, secularization and for many people in the developing nations also Christianization in the sense of proselytizing.

    2.2.1. The inclusion of Christianization as a part of the colonial culture is the historical prejudice of Christians and Christianity and has been a sensitive issue in the formal and informal attitudes of Governments and other religions in those countries.

    2.2.2. Colonialism and its culture has however created its own "antibody" in stimulating nationalism, the fight for national independence, the drive for modernization and the search for national identity.

    2.2.3. To fight the historical prejudice and to participate in the development of nationalism, national independence, modernization process and the building of national identity, Christians have to start with what the Germans call the "Entkultisierung" / "outculturation" (versus "inculturation") of their religion out of the colonial and western culture, so that they are accepted as a trustful partner in the interreligious dialogue. The "Entkultisierung" / "outculturation" is also needed for the smooth and efficient process of inculturation.

2.2.4. The process of **"Entkultisierung"** or **"outculturation"** is a sensitive and sometimes painful process for the local church and Christians. It is a process of internal criticism, corrections and tensions. In many cases it has led to extreme attitudes and solutions. Extreme to the right and extreme to the left. It is important to recognize this process of **"Entkultisierung"** even if it is sometimes out of balance, as a transition to a more balanced and better adjusted way in the renewal of the process of **"inculturation"** into the new (post-colonial) national culture and national identity.

2.3. The interreligious dialogue is a dynamic dialogue. Not only that the dialogue itself should be dynamic but it has to take account of the dynamism within the other religions in the relationship between (their) faith and culture.

2.3.1. The relationship between faith and culture in all religions in the West and in the East is developing along the lines of total harmony and unity of faith and culture (in the primitive religions it is called **"cosmic totality"**) moving towards discrepancies and tensions between faith and culture, moving towards antagonism as in the case of secularism, moving towards a new harmony on a more advanced level, in a revival of religious and cultural life.

2.3.2. It is less dynamic in Buddhism and Hinduism but more outspoken in Christianity and Islam. Islam in Indonesia is experiencing what is called the rediscovery of islamic identity in society. The aim of Islam which is to strive to be the state-religion and state-ideology of the nation has been changed to an approach which endeavours to influence the cultural, ethical and religious life of the state, society and of the nation. This revival however does not become fundamentalism.

2.3.3. The task of Catholic Universities is to support and to formulate scientific guidance for the process of **"Entkultisierung"** / **"outculturation"** and the renewal of a more adjusted **"inculturation"** for the local church and Christians. For the benefit of the interreligious dialogue they can assist in analyzing, clarifying and understanding the dynamics within the other religions in the relationship between faith and culture and so to promote fruitful and productive dialogue with full mutual respect and understanding.

2.4. But the interreligious dialogue in a pluralistic and multireligious society as in Indonesia serves not only the aims of understanding, mutual respect and tolerance, it is especially meant to increase awareness of <u>joint responsibility</u> and to come <u>to joint efforts and cooperation in the search for national identity and national culture, in the process of modernization and in the development of people's welfare.</u>

2.4.1. It is based on the assumption that each religion is aiming to develop human values such as peace, justice and solidarity, material as well as spiritual welfare. Also on the assumption that religion/faith is not a private business as in the West nor a poison for society as in the East, but a valuable force in society which motivates people and influences people's awareness for the common good. Religion is for development.

2.4.2. That is why the Western approach or the Eastern approach to religion and interreligious approach are not valuable and cannot be used as guidance. It needs an <u>authentic approach</u> of the peoples and nations concerned. The Catholic Universities are instrumental in developing this authentic approach to interreligious dialogue aimed at developing joint awareness and responsibility, joint approach and cooperative efforts of the nation concerned.

2.4.3. The founding Fathers of the Indonesian Nation and State have formulated the five principles or **"PANCASILA"** as the state ideology and the philosophy of national unity and solidarity. The five principles are: the Belief in God, Humanity, Unity, Democracy and Social Justice.

2.4.4. Late President Soekarno, one of the Founding Fathers and the one who formulated the Pancasila, said that Pancasila was derived from values that are found in the tradition of all races, people and in the teachings of all religions in Indonesia. It is the common platform for all to join and participate in the National life and development. Pancasila is also the guiding principle in the process of modernization, in the process of economic, social and political development and in the search and building of the national identity and culture.

2.4.5. The tasks of religions in the national development and modernization based on Pancasila are:
a) To safeguard and promote human values in the development process, because the Indonesian National development program is value-based.
b) To strengthen the moral, ethical and spiritual framework of the development.
c) To develop joint responsibility and cooperation in safeguarding and promoting human values and in strengthening the moral, ethical and spiritual framework. Religion for Development.
It is to be a joint effort, not only efforts made by each religion on its own. It is a joint responsibility towards society, the nation and the state. This joint responsibility is the basis and the reference point of the inter-religious dialogue in Indonesia.

II. THE TASK OF THE UNIVERSITIES IN THE DIALOGUE BETWEEN FAITH AND CULTURE IN A PLURAL AND MULTIRELIGIOUS SOCIETY.

1. It is clear that the task of the Universities in the dialogue between faith and culture is not just that of a <u>mediator</u>. Especially <u>not</u> as they are functioning in the secularized culture in the West. It is more than the task of a mediator. Their task is promoting, guiding and animating the dialogue, especially the dialogue with other faiths behind the cultures.
The tasks more traditionally assigned to them are teaching, educating and researching.

2. Moreover the Universities are also agents of change, agents of modernization and agents of development. For new nations, culture means development. A dialogue between faith and culture is for them a dialogue between faith and development. The interreligious dialogue is aimed at religion(s) for development. It goes beyond the traditional definition and tasks of Universities and beyond the Western concept of Universities.

3. It is worthwhile to repeat here what was enumerated as objectives of Catholic Institutes of higher learning in the regional conference of Rectors of South East Asia Catholic Universities in Manila, 1977:

   3.1. To offer qualitatively excellent training and research programmes in all scientific disciplines, which can contribute to a lessened economic dependence upon the developed countries, by enabling the country to exploit, process, control, manage, and trade its own natural resources.

   3.2. To make (interdisciplinary) studies of local, national and regional languages and cultures, customs, in order to promote the feeling of national belonging and identity and the movement towards self-determination, and to avoid destruction of deeply-rooted values as a result of misinterpreted modernism, without the Catholic university loosing its openness towards other cultures and its adherence to the international character of every Catholic university.

3.3. To search for models of development, which focus upon integral human development. To formulate - in a real effort to operationalize the message of the Gospel - development models, which do not only have technical-economic and political-economic dimensions, but contain ethical, cultural, spiritual, moral, and religious dimensions as well and which are aimed at the improvement of the living conditions of everyone.

3.4. To start in its formation from the principle that development is only real if (a) the dignity and worth of the human being is guaranteed; (b) all can profit by material progress; (c) societal and personal development are integrated; and (d) social justice is strived after.

3.5. To form through educational, discussion, exchange, and research-programmes the knowledge and personal attitudes of those concerned in such a way that these theoretical development models can be realized in practice, and to impart a critical stance towards the negative consequences, which technological and industrial development models, which are too one-sided or not well enough considered, might bear for deeply felt social, cultural, religious and spiritual values, and towards the expectation that science and technology alone can satisfy all human needs.

3.6. To function as an academic platform for the Catholic Church, which is served by the Catholic university through (a) a scientific and unbiased study of concrete social, economic, cultural and religious realities; and (b) the formation of laymen, priests and religious, who in one way or another shall be / are involved in development activities of the Church.

3.7. To function as a place of dialogue with representatives of non-Catholic religions and philosophies and to look together for ways in which in mutual cooperation development projects can be started, which give priority to the development of the human being.

3.8. To promote an academic community where students can develop their style and perception of life in an atmosphere of openness and respect for intellectual, religious, social and cultural values not only of their own generation, but of former generations as well, not only of their own culture and ethnic group, but of other cultures and ethnic groups as well.

This encompasses all that is said in this paper about the tasks of Universities in the dialogue between faith and culture in a plural and multi-religious society.

4. This shows the relevance, the necessity and the right of existence of Catholic Universities in such societies.

5. What has been done by Catholic and Christian Universities and Institutions of higher learning in Indonesia; what are they doing, and what are they planning to do. Some examples!

+ + + + +

Faith and Culture in confrontation within the Curriculum

by Thomas JACOBS, Dept. of Theology
IKIP Sanata Dharma, Yogyakarta

The present paper confronts me with the difficulty of where to begin or how to start. The specific theme of this panel is formulated as :

"The concepts of person, of ecclesiology, of Christian humanism as they are taught and lived in the various disciplines of contemporary Catholic universities".

And I would like to put this specific theme within the context of the general theme of our meeting. **"The relationships between Christian faith and cultural environments within which the university is situated"**.

Therefore I would like to speak about **"Faith and culture,** especially in their concrete confrontation, **within the university itself,** more specifically within its curriculum, where this encounter between faith and culture "is taught and lived". And then I must say, that properly speaking there is not such an encounter, let alone a confrontation with the "non-Christian cultures" within the teaching system of the university itself. The concrete social life-situation in Indonesia of course means a constant encounter or even confrontation with other religions. We always live among muslims, hindus, buddhists, and especially "Kebatinan" people. And also in some Catholic universities the majority of the students are non-Christians; and in certain places even the majority of the staff. Nevertheless the class-room cannot be called the meeting-place of faith and non-Christian cultures. As for the "secular culture", it is a big question as to how far such a cultural situation exists in Indonesia, in the sense of a "lay, pragmatic, atheistic" culture. Certainly not in a very clear and recognisable form. But even if it did exist, there is also no question of encounter or confrontation within the teaching system itself. The lectures are either professional or typically Christian. Ecumenism (in the broad sense) or dialogue is not common, and for reasons to be explained now.

The third "form" of cultures is called in the invitation paper "totalitarian cultures". We don't like that word in Indonesia, especially not in so far as the internal situation is concerned. But I do think, that it cannot be denied that the government has a very strong hand in the curriculum and teaching system. People might even feel inclined to use here the word "indoctrination" (which, by the way, is not a bad word in Indonesian). Anyhow, if we want to speak about the concrete encounter between faith and culture, more specifically with "cultural environments within which the university is situated", we probably should speak about the compulsory indoctrination program which the government has introduced into the curriculum and teaching system of the universities in Indonesia, including the Catholic universities.

Some historical background

The Indonesian people has been formed through a historical process of integration, which continued over a long time. This process, properly speaking, did not even start until the beginning of the 20th century, when the Indonesian people rose from the ruins of regional and tribal cultures, with all their multiform aspects. The signal for this rising was the beginning of a national movement in the **"Budi Utomo"** ("Noble Endeavour") in 1908.

Until World War II people from different regions still called themselves "peoples": the Javanese, Sundanese, Madurese, Batak people, etc. The appearance of **"Budi Utomo"** started the process of "indonesianisation" for people from different regions. This process is often also called "nationalisation". One very important step in this process was the so called "Sumpah Pemuda" (The oath of the young generation) in 1928: one country, one people, one language: Indonesia! However this process of indonesianisation, or nationalisation or even integration (of the different tribes and regions within the one state of Indonesia) is still going on. And there are still visible weak points in the national unity. So we are still in the process of **nation building**.

Nation and character building

Together with this process of **nation building** there is also going on a process of "mentality building". The more regional mentality has to be changed into an Indonesian or national mentality. This process is generally called **character building**. And only if this process of nation and character building succeeds, will the unity of Indonesia from Sabang to Merauke be safe. Therefore all signs of discord or disunity have to be prevented or to be put aside. Everything that means a threat to "rust en orde" (Dutch for "peace and order") has to be avoided. For if "rust en orde" is in danger, the unity of the country is no longer guaranteed. Especially when those threats come from SARA (abbreviation for "suku, agama, ras, aliran", which means: tribe, religion, race and religious movement), the leading people get nervous. And the reaction against those threats not seldom creates the impression of over-acting.

From this background it is probably understandable if from the side of the government - not only now, but also in the time of Sukarno - certain measures are taken to promote or even to safeguard the process of nation and character building; and this also in the field of education. In the time of Sukarno, political science and civics had to be taught up to the level of high school (SMTA). In the universities, courses had to be given in MANIPOL (=MANIfesto POLitik, a short formulation of the outline of the government's policy, now called GBHN), the essence of which was formulated in USDEK (the Constitution of 1945, socialism à la Indonesia, guided democracy, guided economy and the Indonesian "character").

The indoctrination program

In the time of the "Orde baru" (the "New order" after the communist upheaval in which many young people were involved), this form of national education was estimated insufficient. So a whole revision of the "national curriculum" took place in 1968. Political science and civics were replaced by education in the ethics of Pancasila (PMP = Pendidikan Moral Pancasila), and MANIPOL got the new name of "Pancasila".

All this was apparently estimated still not enough. Starting at the university level the army made a course in "Study of self resilience" obligatory (which had to be taught by somebody with a qualification from the military training school). This is a course in problems of ideology, politics, economy, socio-cultural questions and the national defence.

When Prof. Nugroho became Minister of Education, two new measures were added: (1) a special training was made obligatory (from primary school to university) in the "**Directive for the Living and Performing of the Pancasila**" (Pedoman Penghayatan dan Pengamalan Pancasila = **P-4**); and (2) a new course was introduced called "**Education in the History of the People's Struggle**" (**PSPB**), obligatory up to the level of high school. According to Prof. Nugroho, the aim of the government was not reached with lectures in Pancasila, because he thought it to be too intellectualistic. He hoped that the more affective element would be developed in the **P-4** training (because more operational directives are given in that training).

The impact of the curriculum

With all these different measures, the government hopes to make the younger generation more nationalistic according to the Javanese motto "Melu handarbeni, melu hangrungkebi, mulatsarira, hangrasa wani" (which means: participate in the country, participate in its defense, ready to correct oneself, to be brave). Unfortunately the country very often is interpreted as the government. The consequence of all this is that if the students start thinking not along the lines of the government, they are considered as rebels and not loyal to the country.

Lectures about Pancasila and self-resilience, as well as the **P-4** training, are very often considered by the students as something added from outside, but compulsory. Therefore many of them feel a kind of antipathy against those courses. In general, in Catholic universities, the students take the courses for what they are, without much fuss. In the Catholic milieu the study of Pancasila is even done with some enthusiasm, for reasons to be explained below. On the other hand, the course in self-resilience is felt as being something forced upon them, without real connexion with their study. Both the course on **Pancasila** and the one on self-resilience are often experienced as annoying and boring, all the more so when the teacher is not capable of making it a little attractive; or when the teacher shows himself/herself to be a dictator.

The most clearly felt effect of these courses is that the students get less time and credits for the study they are really interested in. On the other hand, it is difficult to say how far these courses really help the nation and character building. For there is no concrete data about the results of these courses in the total formation of the students. The attitude of loyalty towards the government from the side of most of the students, with not too many demonstrations or protest actions, could possibly be the result of these courses. Anyhow this is what the government wishes. But as we do not know what the real influence is of our instruction on religion and faith, it is difficult to say what really is the impact of the program of indoctrination from the government.

The question

Confronted with the situation as depicted above, the questions posed by this meeting become really very concrete:

- How does my university face up to the pressures of the surrounding culture especially in the sense as I explained it above ?

- How can we avoid the ivory tower approach ? In a certain sense there is no question of an "ivory tower approach", for the whole program is forced upon us, it is obligatory for all universities. Therefore, the real question is this: Do we swallow all this without any reflections (for the sake of a good relationship with the government, especially with the Ministry of Education) or are we trying to formulate a real answer to this "cultural situation" based on our faith?

- What initiatives should be taken, what attitudes, what openness ? All these are concrete practical questions, which are not so easy to answer.

Pancasila

In March 1985 the Indonesian Bishops Conference issued a booklet named "**Umat Katolik dalam Masyarakat Pancasila**" (The Catholic Community within the Pancasila society). This booklet of 99 pages was a kind of practical hand-out to the Catholic community, especially with regard to the problem of the relationship between Church and State in Indonesia. Already in their meeting of 1981 the Indonesian bishops had decided on the publication of a short formulation of the Church's position. And as is explained in the booklet itself, it was a further development of a more or less official statement already issued in 1970. As a matter of fact, from 1952 on, Catholic authors have been publishing all kinds of reflections and considerations about the Indonesia Statephilosophy, called **Pancasila**. More especially the late Prof. Dr. N. Driyarkara, S.J., has written many articles to clarify this problem (in English: **"Pantja Sila and Religion"**, Jakarta 1959).

For the **Pancasila**, which means **"The Five Principles"** (i.e. (1) Belief in one God; (2) just and civilized humanity; (3) Indonesian unity; (4) democracy under the wise guidance of representative consultations; and (5) social justice for all the people of Indonesia), is at the same time a philosophy or world-view and the juridical fundament of the State, which **de facto** has developed into a State-ideology. And it is here that we run into many problems, e.g. the ones mentioned above. For certain persons the implementation of this ideology might already be questionable on definite points. But specifically the fact that this ideology has to be accepted by all the citizens as their life-basis - at least in principle - raises a problem for people who have their only life-basis in faith in Jesus Christ and his Gospel.

Concrete attitudes

In the context of this short introduction it is impossible to explain all the arguments and discussions about the problems already mentioned. In short we can formulate the Catholic standpoint with regard to the **Pancasila ideology** as follows :

Pancasila, which is called "the holy promise of the people", the State-ideology, the world-view and expression of the "character" of the Indonesian people, formulates basic attitudes which enable the people to live together in a free and human way in the State unity of the Republic of Indonesia. Therefore the Indonesian christians are, by their very Christian faith, demanded to engage themselves in the realisation of Pancasila for the welfare of society, with an openness for urging needs, a critical attitude towards "frozen" formulations, and alert to the manipulation of "holy formulae" for the benefit of certain groups or persons.

In concrete this means, that on the one side Pancasila as such has been accepted as a basic human value, which enables the various ethnic, social and religious groups to live together on a commonly accepted basis. On the other hand, there is a very strong awareness that a "holy promise", expressed in a very definite form, can be a dangerous means of manipulation for those in power. It is as the basis for social life, in all its cultural, socio-economic, and religious aspects, that Panca-sila is acknowledged as a high value. But to become a **concrete** value, interpretation and application are necessary.

Following the doctrine of Vatican II, more specifically **Gaudium et spes**, not only the secular state is accepted, but also the principle of secularisation. A distinction is made between an **expression of faith** and a **realization of faith**. The difference between the two is, that in the "expression of faith" the faith as such becomes visible, whereas in what is called a "realization of faith" nothing religious can be seen. Secondly, the meaning of the expression of faith is nothing else than to bring the faith to the fore. The whole realm of religion belongs to that field of expression of faith. Religion in all its aspects, not only of cult but also of doctrine and morals, is finally directed to the realization of faith in profane life. Religion has always a **functional** value. It is directed towards the development of the faith attitude, which realizes itself in the concrete life situation. As such it is not only accepted in Pancasila, but must be acknowledged as an authentic Christian attitude. What is primary, is not religion (Church), but Christian life. For all that is called "profane" belongs to the realization of faith, and it is there that Christian life becomes an existential reality. Therefore the struggle should never be about the place and the rights of the Church, but about human rights in general, both individual and social, and how these can be supported by Christian faith.

Some basic attitudes

"The political community exists for the common good in which the community finds its full justification and meaning, and from which it derives its pristine and proper right. Now, the common good embraces the sum of the conditions of social life by which individuals, families and groups can achieve their own fulfillment in a relatively thorough and ready way" (GS 74). **In concrete** this means the right of labour, of property and the rights of family life. At least in principle all this is guaranteed by Pancasila, but in a pluralistic way. This is also in accordance with the teaching of Vatican II (GS 76). And what is more, "it is in full accord with human nature that juridical-political structures should afford all their citizens the chance to participate freely and actively in establishing the bases of a political community, governing the state, determining the scope and purpose of various institutions, and choosing leaders" (GS 75). In short: **Democracy**. And it should be obvious that within the realm of this socio-political structure the basic Christian attitudes of faith, hope and charity should be realized. For the concrete realisation of this attitude, the social doctrine of the Church gives two basic principles: solidarity and subsidiarity.

But the most fundamental attitude, underlaying these two principles, is the dignity of the human person, both individually or as a group. And it is precisely here that concrete problems often rise. In the political situation, more specifically because of the trauma of the communist revolution in 1965, there is a tendency to interpret the Pancasila almost exclusively in terms of security, even military security. In May of this year, Mr. Oetojo Oesman, chairman of the committee for the government's program for the doctrine of the Pancasila, was again warning against ideologies ruining the "orthodox" interpretation of the Pancasila. Among those ideologies was also mentioned the theology of liberation. And it seems that here, political interests are conflicting with the social concern of the Church. For this reason the Catholic universities don't stand aloof of the government's program, but try to help its realization by writing their own textbooks (acknowledged by the government) to give an authentic Christian interpretation of this specific Indonesian cultural situation.

Deromanization of Faith Expression
in Third World Countries:
Towards a New Pentecost

========================

By Andrew GONZALEZ, FSC
De La Salle University
Manila, Philippines

I shall be very brief and would like to make the following comments:

1. Except for the perceptive paper of Prof. Frans Seda on the Indonesian situation, I have found the presentations excellent as theoretical and analytical pieces but limited in their perspectives and even ethnocentrically Western, including those not from 'the NATO countries", to use Gregory Baum's designation.

2. Running through the papers is a prevailing paradigm (using Thomas Kuhn's definition of this term) on the relations of faith and culture as dialogical, perhaps even dialectical. Most of the presentations have concentrated on the impact of faith on the local culture in what used to be referred to as mission areas. Actually, Seda describes the relations more aptly as a **"two-way traffic"** and as **out**culturation rather than enculturation. As our own scholars in the Philippines have described it, there was domestication of the faith the receiving culture was not merely passive but active, adapting, domesticating, even coping with oppression and domination.

   Rather than speak of a dialogic meeting between faith and culture, we should perhaps do better by borrowing from cultural anthropology and speak of **"cultural diffusion"** with all that this term entails. It strikes me that in accepting the faith, most third world cultures received it **"in the manner of the recipient"**, to use the old Scholastic axiom.

3. My third and last point is this:

   One formulation of the relation between faith and

culture, restated by Marcello Azevedo in his excellent
paper, is to speak of faith as an existential response
by a person situated in a culture-specific context and
to describe the expression of this faith in culturally
conditioned terms. Behind this formulation is a clutching
at essentials, a constant that somehow remains across
various cultural expressions; this reminds me of Aristo-
telian philosophy of nature and a temptation to yield
to the facile distinction between substance and accident.
However, even this paradigm does not hold since the
person himself and his existential response is culture
bound; no two individuals, let alone communities, respond
to the Christian message in exactly the same way because
of differences of history and culture and personality.
In dealing with the diversity of cultures, there does
not seem to be too much of a theoretical problem; it
is the **unity** which is problematic. It is by now clear
that the language of faith, even of doctrinal formulations, is culturally conditioned. Even the existential
response is culturally conditioned by equally culturally
conditioned perceptions. Do we have to settle for a
Wittgensterinian **"family resemblance"** in our use of
the word **"faith"** ? More problematic is the type of
unity feasible in terms of beliefs and practice once
the full impact of inculturation is accepted, as is
mooted by Frans Seda in his paper. How much pluralism
in behavior and creeds is possible given the radical
openness that Arij A. Roest Crollius speaks of ? Various
attempts have been made in the course of the last three
days to describe the relationship in new terms. Julio
Teran Dutari spoke of a mestizo culture in Latin America,
the result of the dialectic. Jean Ducruet used an organic
metaphor, a tree into which new branches are grafted.
Citing Raimundo Pannikar, Ducruet describes the dynamic
relationship in terms of the evolution of belief as
the believing Christian convert makes contact with and
rediscovers his own past cultures, in the case of Pannikar, Brahmanism and Buddhism. In the case of one sister
who was at yesterday's workshop, it was a case of Buddhism
prior to Christianity. Arij A. Roest Crollius prescribes
"anthropological mediation", using as a given one's
prevailing image of God.

To summarize, we need a new paradigm to describe
the relations between faith and culture especially as
we have to deal with Third World countries. This will
mean not only what Leslie Dewart called the dehelleniza-
tion of Christianity but the deromanization of the Christian response and its pluralization of response into
African, Asian, and Latin American as well as Western,

specifically, Roman.

Under this model, the Church, if it will indeed be **Catholic**, will cease to be exclusively Roman as it develops its theology of pluralism. When this happens, a new Pentecost will erupt. And for the new Pentecost to erupt, the Church needs the university and IFCU and meetings such as this one.

* * * * *

HUMAN PERSON, CHRISTIAN HUMANISM, ECCLESIOLOGY

How these items are taught and lived at Latin American Catholic Universities

by Norberto Francisco RAUCH
P.U.C. do Rio Grande do Sul
Porto Alegre, Brasil

1. INTRODUCTION

The explanation of how the notions of HUMAN PERSON, CHRISTIAN HUMANISM and ECCLESIOLOGY are taught and lived at Latin American Catholic Universities will embody a synthetic view of each topic due to the short period of time available. In order to portray accurately the dominant approaches to these subjects, I have asked several Catholic universities to provide relevant, background information. Ideas regarding the themes in discussion are not unanimous. As a matter of fact, we could not expect anything different than that from our academic communities.

In this explanation, the concepts of HUMAN PERSON and CHRISTIAN HUMANISM are interconnected, whereas the concept of ECCLESIOLOGY is discussed on its own.

Professor Odone José de Quadros helped me by summarizing the philosophical part of this paper.

For a deeper technical development of the matter in discussion, classical works should be consulted.

2. HUMAN PERSON AND CHRISTIAN HUMANISM

2.1. Theoretical Aspects

The main tendencies and approaches to the notions of human person and Christian humanism in the several disciplines taught at Latin American Catholic Universities are:

2.1.1. The great line of personalism

In the representation of the notions of human person and Christian humanism, those who emphasize the personalistic approach point out the following:

- the human person as a subject of the action,
- the human person with his spiritual character as a trade mark to his human innerness,
- the human person with the capacity of making himself respected in the external world,
- the human person not being used as a means,
- the human person having a relational openness to others, acting as an interchangeable being.

Therefore, the human person, spiritual innerness made flesh, destined to hope for truth and for good, transcendent and immanent at the same time, with an aim in himself within a relative autonomy, opens interchangeablely to others and to TRANSCENDENCY, reaching, in this way, the plenitude of human person and establishing his communitarian and social traits.

The human person's innerness characterized by a spiritual character is what provides himself his natural need for transcendency and that is what constitutes the human person's perfection. Here we have the foundations of the human being's eminent dignity.

Transcendency is a demand of the human person's nature and when this same transcendency reaches its summit which is Divine Transcendency it is the supposition itself of the human being's dignity.

2.1.2. The line of existential phenomenology

Taking into consideration all that there is in common between personalism and the so-called existential phenomenology, specially that of the Christian existentialists, we emphasize certain points which are stressed in several subjects taught at the Catholic university when presenting the notions of human person and Christian humanism.

The human person is pictured as consciousness-in-the-world -with-a-body-and-with-the-others.

The trait of a conscious being or of being consciousness is highly stressed. Responsible and free consciousness. Historical consciousness in a given space and time, geography, place, situation. Consciousness capable of love, language, science, art, technology, culture, tradition, history, values and ideals.

Consciousness marked by finitude, precariousness, weakness, contingency, death.

Man pictured as consciousness appears marked by his being-in-the-world: worldliness; being-with-a-body: corporality and being-with-the-others: otherness characteristics.

As human person is pictured as consciousness-in-the-world -with-a-body-and-with-the-others, and as human dignity appears as a result of the free and responsible nature of his same consciousness, "limit situations" or "fundamental situations" of human experience such as: struggling, suffering, sinning and dying are emphasized.

There are also those who prefer the debate of subjects such as: hope, fidelity, love, mystery and commitment.

2.1.3. The line of interdisciplinary phenomenological realism

Contributions from other areas of human knowledge such as physical anthropology, anthropometry, psychology, zoology and others, permit some thinkers the presentation of the person from an interdisciplinary point of view. This occurs, concisely, as follows:

At first sight, the human being looks like an animal, but as a worsened animal. Yes, as an animal because according to certain studies presented by the branches of knowledge previously cited, that which distinguishes the animal is what is called "highly specialized instinct", the animal develops its own vital cycle spontaneously by repeating, through the ages, a biologically inherited behaviour that it acquires from his own species.

In view of this, the human being does not possess highly specialized instincts but only generical instincts, which are common to all the other species such as: the conservation instinct, the defense instinct, the sexual instinct, etc. Because of that, while the animal repeats, man, each man, is a new start.

Therefore, the human being appears as a worsened animal, and in the competition for survival, he ought to have disappeared from the planet's surface a long time ago.

But the opposite has happened: man has imposed himself over animals much stronger than he has dominated nature turning it into his own "habitat", has over-populated the planet and already navigates in the interstellar space.

There can only be an explanation to these facts: there is something in the human being which distinguishes him and this something can only be something extra: rationality.

From this point on, the discourse about the human person goes on within the same orientation and scheme of other tendencies or anthropological approaches.

2.1.4. The line which accentuates otherness

This is the approach which focuses the person within the relationship I-YOU.

This broad approach permits profound reflections about the dialogical trait of the person, his openness to others without taking from the other his freedom and his independence, without melting into the other and without melting the other into the I: the person's traits of interdependence and intersubjectivity.

It is an approach which provides enormous profoundness for the discussion of themes such as: human relationships, interpretation, friendship, love, faith, justice, contingency and Transcendency. It emphasizes qualities such as: interest, respect, originality, openness, acceptance, solidarity, authenticity, inventiveness, communion and encounter.

The whole relationship of otherness is essentially described as a dynamic process, in which two take part and which is built, conquered and done without a final end, during which its participants reach, gradually, their best I, their true I, their "autos", in the relationship with the other and for the other.

2.1.5. The line which emphasizes the social and the liberator character of the other

Sponsored by the approach sometimes called "popular philosophy" and at other times called "liberation philosophy", a type of concept of person less anthological and more praxiological than the others appears and in this concept man is defined through his social, cultural, political and geographical relations and also through his work relations and power relations, through his social tasks, through his being of praxis rather than through his nature and constitution of person.

Within this perspective at the Catholic university there sometimes appears a notion of person which intends to be the real description of the third world person or, at least, of the person in Latin America.

Assuming that the philosophies of the Old World have organized their systems and have succeeded in explaining the totality which included only European reality but not the reality of those who were not included in that social and historical context, the presenters of this approach point out the third world and Latin American person as the "outsider" - the exterior - of large systems mostly Europeans but extensive to those of North America.

The totality of the being to the European conception does not include the third world being. Therefore, it would not be totality. The same can be said about the North American concept.

The whole task relates then to the unfolding of a reflection about this non-being in Latin America: a non-being that neverless exists. The third world and Latin American being. The goal is to give shape to this being in order to set him free.

It is easy to transpose the faces of European thinkers to the faces of the colonizers, be they those of the Old World or the present ones from North America. There is a confrontation between the being and the totality of the colonizers with the non-being -exteriority -which is that of the colonized.

Then the reflection seems to become fertile entering into the concepts of dependency, oppression, domination, exploitation, self-determination, human rights and liberation.

126

The classes which eminently seem to personify this non-being, that therefore exists, are evoked: the poor, the worker, the woman, the Negro, the Indian, these in misery, the oppressed, the colonized, the child, the farmer, the slum-dweller, the wage earner, the popular classes, the people.

Therefore it is an approach which tries to produce a philosophical discourse about the person having as a starting-point Latin American reality at the end of the twentieth century, an age described as one of "extreme oppression" which has been compared to the end of the eighteenth century "when many heroes and martyrs started to become aware of the necessary emancipation".

Those who have chosen this approach to the notion of person to work with in the classroom are aware of the not very well limited boundaries which certain applications of the thematic to the praxis can present. It is a completely committed understanding of the person and that is why many times this approach has led to use much more sociological-political -economical-cultural proceedings, some other times it has led to disentangling itself from similar ideologies and at other times it is easily mixed with lines of thought which have already presented the final solution for the history of mankind a certain time ago.

2.2. Aspects of the Experience of the Human Person and Christian Humanism Notions at Catholic Universities in Latin America

Over the last years, Catholic universities in Latin America have mainly worried about their own identity. The three subjects we are discussing at the moment, human person, Christian humanism and ecclesiology integrate, in a very direct and essential way, this identity. Practically, Catholic universities have undertaken, some more intensively than the others, the following proceedings and activities:

- Elaboration of a Declaration of Principles or other reference documents more or less equivalent or complementary to each other: Reference Guidelines, Doctrinary Guidelines, Philosophy of the Institution, Pedagogical project.

- Adoption of special strategies in the selection of academic and general staff in order to establish an identification between them and the fundamental objectives and compromises of the Institution. At my University, Pontifical Catholic University of Rio Grande do Sul, we have designed a form specifically for those who are applying for a teaching position. This is called "Perfil do Professor da PUCRS" (an Outline of PUCRS' Professors). It does not limit itself to aspects of professional competency, it also deals with aspects of the human person, Christian humanism and their consequences.

- Organization of interinstitutional seminars aiming at thinking about the subjects we are presently discussing.

- Accomplishment of activities related to each institution in particular such as: programmes of continued education for the chairman board as well as for the academic and general staff; creation of interdisciplinary groups specifically designed for the university pastoral and for reflection.

- Accomplishment of activities designed to develop mutual fraternity. Some of them are: "reception" of new students and professors at the University; associative lunches and dinners with the academic staff, meetings of university directors, the practice of sports by students, professors and general staff.

- In what refers to the academic curriculum of graduate courses, most Catholic Universities offer a number of courses, some designed for the whole students community, some which are specific for certain colleges, with the aim of deepening the knowledge and the consciousness in what concerns the human person, Christian humanism and the religious phenomenon. Referring again to my own university, I cite subjects of general education which are offered to all students. They are: Philosophy, Sociology, Religion and Studies of Brazilian Problems. Naturally, it is not enough to offer those courses. We must take care so that they have an adequate orientation.

- At life experience level, students and the academic staff associate in a series of humanistic programmes designed to attend individuals who belong to the lower classes. It would be too long to cite all fields in which Catholic universities act; some are: medicine, dentistry, law, social assistance, psychology, engineering, education, agricultural studies and so on.

- Finally, we, systematically, use publications and communication means both internal and external to spread knowledge and to increase awareness and compromise in what regards the three topics we are discussing at the moment.

3. ECCLESIOLOGY

In the analysis of the ecclesiology which is taught and lived in Latin America today, we have to take into consideration Vatican Council II (1962-1965), the Second General Latin American Episcopal Conference (1968) in Medellin, Colombia, the Third General Latin American Episcopal Conference (1979) in Puebla, Mexico; it is also necessary to have in mind Latin American social reality as well as the development of the Liberation Theology.

We do not want to forget or get away from other concepts of ecclesiology but the concept which has produced more profound changes is that of CHURCH, PEOPLE OF GOD. This concept involves a higher recognition, participation and responsibility of the Christian layman in the church. Consequently, it means less clericalism. More, or, at least as important as that, is the communitarian notion which this ecclesiology embodies, since the people have a common commitment with a project, with a journey of solidarity. It reminds us of the history of the Jews which is narrated in Exodus. The Church viewed as PEOPLE OF GOD has a commitment with TRANSCENDENCY through FAITH and a SECULAR compromise with REALITY and its TRANSFORMATION.

The two-sided facet of FAITH and SECULARITY is strongly supported by the LIBERATION THEOLOGY. It has its origins in the analysis of Latin American reality in confrontation with the demands of the Gospel. While the latter preaches love, fraternity, justice and liberty, the REALITY of the continent is marked by enormous social diversity, social injustice and dependency.

Even being the largest Catholic continent in the world, Latin America does not portray properly in its organization and social structure life living with five hundred years of Christianism.

The two-sided ecclesiastical nature: spiritual and secular which are often also called vertical and horizontal generates, in every day life, tensions in and out of the clergy, due to the difficulties of the social-political-economical reality. The episcopate recognizes the problem publicly when it states in Puebla: "...This social situation has brought tensions into the very heart of the church: tensions which were produced by groups which emphasize "the spiritual side" of their mission resenting their social promotion work or by groups determined to transform the mission of the church in mere work of human promotion." (Puebla, A Evangelizaçâo no presente e no futuro da América Latina, Ed. Loyola, 1979, pp. 108-109).

Among the people and in the mass media, terms such as PROGRESSIVE and CONSERVATIVE are often used.

Tensions between the clergy and structures outside the clergy are a result of this clear and preferential option, although not exclusive, of Latin American Church for the poor and oppressed and this option does not match dominant social-political-economical interests.

Even inside the Church itself there are groups, as it is the case of the "Cristandades" that would like to see the Church closer to its spiritual commitment and away from social conflicts.

Latin American Church, ad intra, in spite of the divergencies it faces, gives us magnificent examples of fraternity and of group pastoral: episcopal conferences, fraternal dioceses, clergymen conferences, meetings, laymen movements and so on.

The concept of PEOPLE OF GOD gives the Church an institutional and structural trait of a higher communitarian scope, with distribution of functions and responsibilities following the expression of the General Episcopal Conference at Puebla.

It is understandable why this notion is not established by a decree to be immediately followed for it consists of a process.

We can ask ourselves: How do university students react to this notion of ecclesiology?

There is no doubt that, generally speaking, Latin American academic communities admire and support the secular-social-political commitment of the Church specially in what regards the defense of the poor, oppressed and of those who suffer from injustice.

The university pastoral is much more accepted and causes many more effects when this commitment is stressed.

Nevertheless, in the large university group, enthusiasm, adhesion and experience of the FAITH commitment and of communitarian values is not noticeable.

This fact appears with more intensity among popular classes and in particular at basic ecclesiastic communities.

Besides the notion of CHURCH, PEOPLE OF GOD which we have been expousing up to now, it is equally important to refer to the notion of CHURCH, WORK OF THE HOLY SPIRIT. This concept serves as the basis and it also encourages some ecclesiastical movements in Latin America which are called Charismatic Movements and which are very significative and numerous. They exist in and out of the Catholic Church.

In spite of the dynamism and of the great number of signs of hope which exist in the Latin American Church, we cannot disregard the multiple aspects of secularization nor of dechristianization of the culture nor the flourishing of sects.

I finish the present discussion referring to "Gaudium et Spes" and to Puebla when discussing about Catholic universities: "Its main educational mission is the promotion of an integral culture capable of educating people who will stand out through their deep humanistic and scientific knowledge, "through a testimony of faith when facing the world" (GE 10); through the practice of a sincere Christian morality and through the commitment of creating a more fraternal and just Latin America (Puebla, 1060, Ed. Loyola, 1979, p. 292).

+ + + + +

The concepts of person and Christian humanism as they are taught in S. Indian Colleges

by Sr. Stella Maria
Xavier Board of Higher Education
Bangalore, India

The situation in India is much different from many Western universities. We are living in the midst of people who follow other religions. Therefore the concept of person from the Christian perspective is not directly treated in most of the Universities, except in the Catholic faculties or seminaries and a few chairs of Christianity established in certain universities.

However India has developed its own concept of person which penetrates the whole curriculum of studies in the university. The classical (the traditionally and religiously valid) understanding of man in India is different from that of the West. The West defines man as "a rational animal" and calls him a person. India designates man as "ātman", a word which is used also for designating God or "Brahman". In the definition "rational animal", rationality reflects the Divine and man becomes a person as he participates in the divine nature of self-reflection. In the Indian vision of man he was first conceived as a member of the divine family and then was distinguished from it with an additional note of possessing a body, subject to life and death. Hence he was called Jivātman.

In the contemporary literature that is taught in the university classes there is a considerable influence from the West, and a new concept of person as an agent of activity and achievement is now being evolved. In developing the concept of a full-fledged person, India developed the "way of accomplishment" (pravrtti - Marga) and the "way of retirement" (nivrtti - Marga). Usually what ordinary people, including university students, understand by person is the person of achievements and success in the world: a self-made man. The "way of retirement" is a way of returning to one's own inner self, going beyond the achievements in the world and establishing harmony and order in all phases of life. Though this is not directly treated in the class rooms, a long tradition of Hindu and Buddhist religions has left this as a precious ideal in the culture and consciousness of the people. Hence the movements of Ahimsa, Transcendental Meditation, etc. which originated in Indian soil.

Christian humanism in Malayalam Literature

The second topic I propose for discussion in this session is Christian humanism. I present a few ideas on Christian humanism as it is communicated through the literature of one of the South languages, namely Malayalam, in the Colleges of Kerala. Malayalam language is the medium of instruction at the school level except in the English medium schools and is taught as a language, both at the school and university levels. It has a rich literary tradition expressed in the forms of novels, poems, films, dramas and literary criticism. The themes expounded in many of these works are profoundly human, touching on relevant social problems and moral values. Though written by many non-Christian authors their messages have much in common with the basic ideas affirmed by Christian humanism. The dignity of the human person, his communion with nature and the transcendent, his social rights and responsibilities, concept of woman and motherhood, autonomy of the secular, struggle between good and evil, experience of pain and joy, search for the unreachable... all find touching treatment in these varied works. They provide an excellent opportunity for the teacher to lead the youth through the paths of elevated reflection and personalized value formation. I shall illustrate this through a brief analysis of one or two typical works.

Keshava Devu - A modern novelist of Kerala, Hindu by religion

A reputed novelist in Malayalam literature through his novel "Odayilninnu" - the title could be translated into English as "From the Gutter" - very powerfully conveys the two great Christian humanistic values: (1) the dignity of the human person - in the midst of stark poverty and social degradation; (2) the Christian idea of self-gift as the highest form of freedom.

The hero Pappu - the son of an agricultural tenant - driven by poverty, leaves school and begins to earn a living. He takes to rikshaw pulling, a means of transport for short distances in rural areas which is no longer in vogue. One day his rikshaw dashes with a child on the street and throws her down into a gutter. Pappu, deeply moved, takes the fatherless child home and brings her up. He works harder still to send her

to school and give her a comfortable life. By this time
he becomes a tuberculosis patient. Yet he does not bow
his head before any rich man or take to begging for
his daily sustenance. He takes to less strenuous work
and finds peace and happiness in his, though poor,
independent style of life. It is here we find the strength
and undaunted courage of the personhood of man, who
falls back upon the inner resources of his mind. Pappu,
the hero, reminds us of W. Wordworth's poem "The Leech
- Gatherer or Independence" where the old man, bent
with age and disease, still earns an independent living,
by gathering leeches and selling them. The novel ends
with the orphan girl marrying a man of comfortable means
and Pappu makes his self-gift complete by disappearing
from the scene, leaving them to their new-found happiness.
Pappu's dry, weak cough dies out, as he moves away to
unknown distances. A parallel to Pappu is found in Jean
Valjean, the hero in Victor Hugo's famous novel "Les
Misérables".

This novel "From the Gutter" prescribed for university students of Kerala has a tremendous impact on
the youth who are so much influenced by to-day's mass
media and the values they proclaim.

Balamaniamma - Living Poet

We in India living in a multi-religious, multi-
cultural context do not have a Catholic university,
but our universities do not belittle Christian humanistic
values. To illustrate my point, I would again refer
to a Hindu author, this time a woman writer, still living,
whose poems are prescribed for the three universities
in Kerala. Her name is Balamaniamma and I would very
briefly refer to two of her poems: "The Cradle" and
"the Swing", both glorifying motherhood and childhood.
In these two poems the author develops a consistent
ethic of life: that all human life, from conception
to death, is a wondrous gift from God; because it is
sacred, individuals and society have an obligation to
protect and nurture human life at every stage of its
development. To-day when we are challenged with the
evils of abortion, discrimination against the female
child, euthanasia, sex determination, etc. these poems
emphasize the sanctity of human life and strongly negate
the many threats to it in our world today. The author
is fully convinced of the words of the poet - I quote
again Wordsworth - speaking of child "Trailing clouds
of glory do we come from God who is our home".

Christian Humanism

There is a strong tendency among the contemporary students to give themselves to values than to religion. This is partly on account of the waves of secularization flooding the country and partly because of the revival of religious fundamentalism and fanaticism. Students are very often exploited by the fanatic groups of people, be it in religion, politics or social factors. As a result, a substantial number of intelligent students become indifferent to religion as such, but take interest in genuine human values. In the Indian situation this may not be named as Christian humanism, but in fact it is a sort of Christian humanism, if we remember the expression of Karl Rahner: the anonymous Christian.

The situation becomes, sometimes, tense when the religious authorities do not welcome the new trends of Christian humanism. This is an area in which new researches could be undertaken, namely how could we evolve certain norms to judge the genuineness of a movement, which does not follow the traditional religious methods, but stands for real human values and ideals.

+ + + + +

FINAL SUMMARY

by Guillermo Rodriguez-Izquierdo
Universidad Pontificia de Comillas
Madrid, Spain

Note: Reports given during the Assembly are indicated here within brackets with the two first letters of the reporter's name (Az = Azevedo; Ba = Baum; Cr = Crollius; Du = Ducruet; Se = Seda).

The first title planned as the topic for our General Assembly had been "**Education in faith within a pluri-cultural society**". In fact, this proposal aimed at identifying and explaining the significance of our presence in the modern world. In Western countries, the ancient Catholic tradition has been swallowed up by a new scientific view of the world and by a new humanistic view of history and society. In countries with other traditions, particularly in countries which are becoming aware in this century of new ideas in development, a modern way of facing the world and society seems to be appearing. Faced with these conditions, does it still make sense that the training of the younger generation be based on preconceived Christian ideas? Are our universities creating citizens adapted to their social environment or, on the contrary, are the very ideals of our universities today out of touch with our modern world?

During the meetings of the IFCU Administrative Council, we felt the need to reword the title in order to express our central concern and avoid certain disadvantages found in the present formulation. The words "**education in faith**" seemed in fact to suggest the idea of indoctrination which was contrary to the intentions of those who had proposed the topic for the Assembly. The title as restated - "**Faith and Culture: the role of the Catholic university**" - puts more importance on the relationship between faith and culture; this question which has appeared several times in Church documents

as the constant concern of the post Conciliar Church
is undoubtedly an example of what was called after the
Council the "new conscience of the Church" or the "new
Church psychology". We had therefore proposed and taken
on this new formulation in the hope not only of touching
on a sensitive issue and of suggesting an important
task for our universities, but also in the hope of
locating within this "sensitive issue" one of the keys
to the "raison d'être" of Catholic universities as such.
The new title, at the same time, opened up much broader
perspectives to us. Our horizons have now been broadened,
it is certain, but nevertheless, we would not want to
lose sight of our initial concern which is now incorporated in a more general theme.

As is always the case in these reports, we run
the risk that our theoretical statements represent ideas
which are very lofty but so far removed from reality
that they can only be used as general guidelines. Those
here who know at close hand the reality of our work,
understand to what extent the ideals must take shape
through discussions and practical work until they succeed
in permeating our daily activities. In stressing the
concrete tasks indicated in the reports, we notice that
a large part of them depend on the competence of those
who make up the organizational nucleus of a Catholic
university, along with the group of Catholic professors
sharing the same ideals and the Theology Departments
or sections more professionally committed in subjects
directly related to faith. Other tasks have also been
mentioned which pertain to us all and with which we
all can identify, even the non-Catholic professors and
students.

In the present summary, I intend to sum up the
following points:

1. Principles discussed in the addresses made to the
   Assembly.

2. Directions for implementing these principles.

3. Concrete tasks suggested to the Catholic universities,
   distinguishing between:

   3.1. Those which specifically concern the organizers
        of the university, the Catholic professors and
        students as well as the Theology Departments
        or Sections.

3.2. Those which concern all members of our universities, including non-Catholic professors and students.

1. PRINCIPLES - SIZE OF THE TASK

This first point is stated in very general terms. I will begin by summarizing the way in which our speakers dealt with the relationship between faith and culture and an ecclesial task. Then I will deal with how to implement concretely this mission in our universities.

Marcello Azevedo defined the topic in very precise terms. Can Christianity, the Christian faith and message have meaning for the present-day world? Can they survive today? In today's cultural framework can they find not only conditions for existing side by side, whether in tolerance or opposition, but even conditions for growth which allows for mutual criticism and integrated dialectics.

Dealing with the question of the Church's role in a dialogue with the world, we could ask ourselves under what circumstances this dialogue would be authentic and would lead to reconciliation. Must the Church change its attitude? Must it change its way of speaking? Must it try to change the world so that the world will understand it? What must be its goal: create a new cultural climate as a receptive atmosphere for Christianity (Az), or on the contrary, integrate Christianity into the cultural climate or climates which prevail in the world today?

Frans Seda gave us a very clear analysis of five attitudes which it is possible to adopt in the relationship between Christianity and culture. In addition, he stressed that inculturation, which is the official position of the Magisterium after Vatican II, must take place in a two-way manner, not only in one way leading to penetration and integration. It is important, it seems to me, to insist on the fact that this bilateral aspect of the dialogue means that there are two speakers, the Church and the world; that each of them must fulfil a double function: listen and speak. Thus the double game of the dialogue takes place: to give and to receive. Let us analyse it point by point.

On the one hand, the Church must listen, that is to say, a part of its vocation is the wish to know the world as it is; the Church tends to move toward the world, to analyze it, to study it, to understand it. The Council spoke to us about this by using the fortunate expression: "the signs of the times". But the Church must also speak, in a way that is adapted to the present-day world, in order to be properly interpreted and properly understood. When mentioning this dialogue, Ecclesiam suam stressed the second aspect, to speak the language of our time, much more than it did the first, to learn about the world (Cr).

Both aspects have interested the Church and the two have been integrated into various ecclesial documents. Evangelii nuntiandi, for example, when listing the tasks of local Churches, stresses the need of a theological formulation appropriate to the circumstances surrounding each place and each time (1). Jean Ducruet spoke to us explicitly about this when he discussed the relationship between dogmatic formulas and theologies on the one hand, and cultural plurality on the other. And he added that theologies are learned by conditioning and are relative. He mentioned in this same context the limitations and inaccuracies of language when expressing our faith, as well as our restricted possibilities for conceptualization by which we receive a transcendent reality, of another order. Jean Ducruet also stressed that the evangelical message, differing acording to cultures, must be expressed within the framework of a faith where the words and events as revealed by God must be repeatedly reconsidered, reformulated and relived within each human culture.

Frans Seda insisted on the importance of a dialogue between religions, on the need to go beyond the attitude of antagonism with regard to other religions and that of the unique and perfect character of the Christian message, so that we can progress toward an open approach which can contemplate the extent of grace in other religions and recognize that these can really be chosen by God as media salutis. In an article published several years ago, Father Daniélou made the remark that Christianity must assume, purify and transform elements from other religions (2).

In all this dialogue, suggested Roest Crollius, the Church has a worthwhile and positive message to transmit to our world today because, according to Gaudium et spes, "the Christ, who is the New Adam, in the very revelation of the mystery of the Father and of his love, makes man fully manifest to himself" (GS 22). There

comes out of Christianity a humanism which contemplates
the mystery of man in a completely different dimension,
with an eschatology which includes the categories of
man's origin and perspective, as well as those of
conflict, commitment and hope.

Finally, the address of Gregory Baum pointed out
that this dialogue must go beyond the simple framework
of intellectual elements in theological formulations,
in order to become as well, and especially, itself a
contrast with the social and political reality of our
world. Christian humanism is also the coming of new
men capable of facing today's socio-political problems.
Marcello Azevedo was of the same opinion.

2. DIRECTIONS - ATTITUDES TO THE DIALOGUE

In this section I propose to reconsider several
suggestions made before the Assembly on the tone, attitude
and style which must characterize this dialogue. I will
no longer limit myself, as in the preceding section,
to the Church's problems in general, but I will also
speak of the specific attitude to be adopted by Catholic
universities as they face the task which awaits them.

The question is important and it has been well
broached, at least since the Council openly raised the
question of relationship between the Church and the
present-day world. During the discussion on the plan
of the pastoral constitution "The Church in the world
of our time", Mgr. Wojtyla, then archbishop of Cracow,
speaking in the name of all Polish bishops, had said:
"The Church does not have to instruct non-believers.
It must search jointly with the world. Thus, one would
avoid the ecclesiastic tone of this plan and all the
lamentations with regard to the world. Let us avoid
any monopolizing spirit and any moralizing spirit. One
of the greatest weaknesses of this plan is that it makes
the Church appear authoritarian" (3). Already at the
time of the Council, the future John Paul II attached
great importance to the tone used by the Church in its
dialogue with the world. It is a theme of greatest
importance also for Catholic universities, which in
general must carry on their dialogue with other universities and cultural milieux in the common field and
language of science. Based on the premise, acquired
through academic merit, of being a scientific inter-
locutor, a broader dialogue can be pursued where faith
has its say.

In this respect, the following are some important remarks made at our General Assembly.

1. Roest Crollius indicated that the attitude of openness would avoid having the ideal become hardened into ideology and avoid having the cultural identity of our Catholic universities become a caricature of a cultural apartheid. Isolation can be a great obstacle to dialogue, whether it be in the form of religious exclusivity, cultural apartheid or exaggerated specialization. This isolation can also result from ideological choices being imposed from inside or outside the university; the dialogue then is transformed into a struggle for academic freedom, a necessary stipulation for academic creativity.

I add here also the remark of Marcello Azevedo according to which the university has, as vocation and obligation, to know the modern world and to know itself. From this stems the need for interdisciplinarity, dialogue, and a critical attitude with regard to one's own docility to modern culture; and all this through analyses founded on the basic presuppositions of modern times.

2. Frans Seda spoke of the necessity of "deculturate" in order to "inculturate" and indicated that inculturation is the official attitude of the magisterium after Vatican II. He recalled, on the one hand, the disadvantages of including Christianization as an element of a colonial culture, and, on the other hand, the need, in the dialogue with other religions, to instigate an awareness of joint responsibility, through combined efforts and at the same time collaboration in the search for a national culture.

3. Jean Ducruet stressed the principle of the autonomy of terrestral realities, very justly emphasized by Vatican I and Vatican II. Despite the elementary aspect of this remark, it seems to me to be very necessary, because there is a permanent temptation to return to a certain fundamentalism, to go back at least in part to the fideism and traditionalism of the nineteenth century, to take faith as the point of departure, even when this point should be plain reasoning.

4. Gregory Baum showed us his concern for certain Catholic faculties regarding the risk of real opposition to Church doctrine, even if the president and the

professors present themselves publicly as entirely
Catholic. His analysis seems extremely important to
me. Our universities are involved in the dynamics of
research for success which comes by adopting neo-conservative principles causing us to look toward success
models superior to ours and to forget those that are
behind us. As Gregory Baum very well expressed it:
"Neo-conservative culture tries to reconcile us to
inequality". In other words, it teaches us to accept
the world as it is, without posing the problems of
injustice and inequality, without urging us to change
the world. Rather it invites us to settle in there
comfortably, to profit from the situation in order to
guarantee the success of our institution, the best
positions in social planning and in development for
our students. As for Marcello Azevedo, he stressed the
need for the university to criticise radically the
liberal-capitalist and marxist-communist traditions
within the context of the originality in each situation;
this criticism would permit the discovery of concrete
ways in which Christians could be present in public
life and the awareness of ways in which the political
dimension of the Christian faith could fulfil its
mediatory role. This is intimately tied to the relationship between the university and the real world and would
not be limited to simple relations between "university
and business". The university cannot isolate itself
from the context of poverty and oppression which surrounds
it, nor from our world in general; it must show its
political sensitivity in the face of urgent social
transformations (Az).

3. TASKS SUGGESTED TO THE CATHOLIC UNIVERSITIES

**3.1. Tasks which specifically concern the organizers
of the university, the Catholic professors and students
as well as the Theology Departments or Sections.**

The theme of our Assembly allowed for a good number
of practical suggestions under this heading. Here are
some of them:

1. Need to liberate Church history from all
narrowness and partiality: privileges of orthodoxy,
of uniformity, of established Christianity, of the
clerical aspect, of its Western character (Du).

2. Hermeneutics of Magisterium declarations in
their historical context (Du).

3. Theological formulation in various cultural contexts: many ways to express the same faith. Problems posed by such creativity in the framework of accepted and established theological formulations and languages (Du). Need to expand the dialogue to the context of modern sciences in order to see what the possibilities for reformulation are, taking into account languages accepted as scientific (Az), and the need to discover in each case the languages that are susceptible to being used for theological formulation (Du). Religious background in diverse languages (Du).

4. Dialogue with other religions: some very valuable elements of this dialogue were pointed out to us by Frans Seda and Jean Ducruet in their respective addresses. Working from an attitude that can conceive of other religions as _media salutis_, as instruments of grace, we must ascertain which aspects can be picked up, purified and transfigured, according to the Daniélou formula, in order to express our faith. The dialogue faith-religion-cultures must also be a dialogue of the religions of the world, of religions among themselves and an inter-religious dialogue, that is, a dialogue of different religions within the heart of the believer (Du, Se).

5. Presentation of Christianity in academic language, in the form of university course offerings on Christianity which might interest Christians and non-Christians (Cr).

6. Clarification of the relationships between religion and development, Christianity and participation in public life, Christianity and cultural identity (Se). Relation to national and regional languages.

7. Discovery of the scientific and prophetic language in which the Church's and our universities' interest might be expressed concerning matters of social restructuration and social and political participation, while going beyond any sense of it being based on successful neo-conservative positions. Assimilation of preferential options for the poor, and research on all that this might mean in the various disciplines (Ba).

8. Promotion of an academic community in which students can develop a style and perception of life in an atmosphere of openness and respect for intellectual,

religious, social and cultural values, not only of their own generation but also of preceding generations; not only of their own culture and ethnic group but also of other cultures and ethnic groups (Se).

9. Identification of new forms of Christian spirituality within the framework of the tension between the traditional forms of spirituality and the life of people in the electronic age (Cr).

10. Articulation of new forms of thought and praxis, on one hand, and of faith and life, on the other, going beyond the viewpoint of liberal-capitalist over-simplification (what is religious is not scientific) and that of Marxist-communist over-simplification (the only valuable force for change is that which comes from dynamic materialism). Discovery of and prominence given to the forces capable of integrating and transforming the Christian faith (Az).

As a personal reflection, I would like to mention briefly my own reactions to these ideas, especially in relation to the mission and responsibility of theology professors. Theologians are very often ignored by the scientific community. This can be due in part to the simplifications used by experts and men of science to judge everything which seems unscientific to them, but it can come equally from a certain distance in the work methods of theologians. Many theologians still have the tendency to work alone, rather than in a team; they have in mind only the writing of <u>their</u> book or <u>their</u> research articles, of directing the work of <u>their</u> students on various subjects. It would indeed be necessary, in my opinion, to encourage theologians to work as a team amongst themselves and with experts from other disciplines, in order to have greater interdisciplinary exchange. The history of science has considerably influenced the history of philosophy, beginning with the seventeenth century; it has influenced much less, it seems to me, the history of theology. The latter has always tried to give an answer to questions asked by philosophy and the sciences; today we need to initiate new ways. As a comparison, here is an example of what we wish to say. Just as everywhere in Latin America, theology has given rise to an impressive movement of integration into social and cultural reality, in the same way this cultural integration must extend also to the new culture created by science and technology in specifically academic circles. The development of local theologies was discussed; as we have already mentioned, _Evangelii nuntiandi_ entrusts to the local Churches the task of theological formulation, not of course as a breaking apart of Church and theology, but, on the contrary, as a deeper incarnation of Church and theology into various cultural contexts. Science is the cultural framework of the scientific community. We must reach it from our own world, by bringing to it the entire evangelical message. I do not mean by this that theology must speak in the formal language of the positive sciences, but we must be well aware of the fact that, in our day, formalization has changed the cultural substrata of all sciences; consequently, theologians can no longer do their work by isolating themselves in their corner, far away from the influences of the outside world.

3.2. **Tasks which concern all of us, including non-Catholic students and professors who work in our universities.**

1. Studies of local reality (languages, customs, values). Avoid destruction of values (cultural ecology). Revalorization of peoples' identity (Se).

2. Elaboration of complete development models which incorporate ethical, cultural, spiritual, moral and religious values, with emphasis put on the dignity and value of the human being, universal outreach (development for all), integration of social and personal development, search for social justice and criticism of the negative aspects of development (Se).

3. Constant encouragement of scientific dialogue at the highest level and exchanges with universities of differing backgrounds; integration into the national and international scientific community (Cr - Se).

4. Awareness of the value, extent and limits of science and scientific methods. Awareness of the Christian way of pursuing activities in medicine, the economy, politics, etc. (Du).

5. Service rendered to society through various forms offered by the university, among others, by courses in lifelong education which is most needed at all times (Cr) and by a knowledge of the social and political reality. In one country, the rector of a Catholic university said to me: "Thanks to studies which we pursued in a continuing manner, our university knows better than the government the elements which mold the socio-

economic reality of our country; that is why they must turn to us". Here is one excellent way in which to render service to the community.

6. Ethics of service and solidarity (Cr).

To these facts drawn from topical speeches given before the Assembly, I would like to add here also my personal reflection which deals particularly with the work of all our professors, Catholic or non-Catholic, in our universities. The cultural context of our world is, as we said earlier, largely scientific and technical. The existence and strength of the scientific community as such is not a new phenomenon in our century, but today this phenomenon has taken on extraordinary breadth and size, to the point that it has assumed completely new characteristics. The scientific method and language have more and more overrun such disciplines as linguistics or psychology which formerly were much more in the category of human sciences. If we want this world which is ours, the academic world, to encompass the Church, to include us as believers, we must know it thoroughly, listen to it, know how to express ourselves in its language. This does not come automatically; success in this comes only through integration, inculturation into the scientific and technological world.. Only by becoming a scientist will a believer be able to express himself in a way that is understood by other scientists. The latter must see in us authenticity and must understand that the Church loves science and is truly concerned with it, that it is not afraid of great freedom in research. Only by sincere dialogue based on clear and sound human exchanges, can the attitudes of one another be understood and accepted. Only human contact will make it possible for believers to be held in estime by scientists; then the dynamics of a pleasant and positive dialogue can come into play. Such is the role which falls to us specifically as Catholic universities in the missionary effort of the Church. It is of greatest importance that our professors, believers or not, establish relations with professors from other universities, that they know their colleagues and are known by them, that they pursue the dialogue without faltering. This role of scientific exchange, research sharing and information in the authentic, stern and difficult context of science is one of the noblest missions that our Catholic universities can accomplish and it will make of them, as our president Michel Falise has so often said, true "laboratories" of the Church.

Notes

(1) Paul VI, <u>Evangelii nuntiandi</u>, n° 63.

(2) J. Daniélou, <u>Christianisme et religions non chrétiennes</u>, in "Etudes", 1966, pp. 325-336.

(3) H. Fesquet, <u>Diario del Concilio</u>, ed. "Nova Terra", Barcelona, 1967, p. 698.

Orders and payments to:

AMMINISTRAZIONE PUBBLICAZIONI PUG/PIB
Piazza della Pilotta, 35 – 00187 Roma – Italia
Tel. 06/678.15.67 – Telefax 06/678.05.88

Conto Corrente Postale n. 34903005 – Compte Postal n. 34903005
Monte dei Paschi di Siena – Sede di Roma – c/c n. 54795.37

Riproduzione anastatica: 15 novembre 1991
Tipografia Poliglotta della Pontificia Università Gregoriana
Piazza della Pilotta, 4 – 00187 Roma